Motorbooks International
MIL-TECH SERIES

AURORA

The Pentagon's Secret Hypersonic Spyplane

Bill Sweetman

First published in 1993 by Motorbooks International Publishers & Wholesalers, PO Box 2, 729 Prospect Avenue, Osceola, WI 54020 USA

Motorbooks International books are also available at discounts in bulk quantity for industrial or sales-promotional use. For details write to Special Sales Manager at the Publisher's address

Library of Congress Cataloging-in-Publication Data
Sweetman, Bill.
    Aurora : the Pentagon's secret hypersonic spyplane / Bill Sweetman.
        p.   cm. — (Motorbooks International mil-tech series)
        Includes index.
        ISBN 0-87938-780-7
        1. Aurora (Reconnaissance aircraft)
I. Title.   II. Series.
    UG1242.R4S94   1993
    358.4'583—dc20   93-14329

Printed in the United States of America

On the front cover: A painting of Aurora by Kerry Leslie.

On the back cover: A joint project of Lockheed and the USAF Flight Dynamics Laboratory from the 1960s, this hypersonic research aircraft bears an uncanny resemblance to the aircraft seen over the North Sea in 1989. *USAF via David Selegan.* A cutaway of the Aurora by Mike Badrocke.

Contents

Introduction **Would Your Government Lie to You?**   4

Chapter 1 **Blackest of the Black**   11

Chapter 2 **Flying Toward Space**   31

Chapter 3 **The Hypersonic Revolution**   64

Chapter 4 **The Price of Denial**   87

           Index   96

Would Your Government Lie to You?

**"Is there anything else to which you would wish
to draw my attention?"
"To the curious incident of the dog in the night-time."
"The dog did nothing in the night-time."
"That was the curious incident."**

–Conan Doyle, *Silver Blaze*

On March 6, 1990, one of the United States Air Force's (USAF) sleek, matte-black Lockheed SR-71 Blackbird spyplanes, serial number 64-17972, shattered the official air speed record from Los Angeles to Washington's Dulles airport. There, a brief snow-dusted ceremony marked the end of the SR-71's operational career, as the record-breaking aircraft was handed over to the National Air and Space Museum.

Officially, the SR-71 was being retired to save the $200–$300 million a year that it cost to operate the fleet. Some reporters were told that the SR-71 had been declared redundant because spy satellites had improved so much that the aircraft was no longer needed.

But there was something badly wrong with the picture: not only was the Air Force, from chief of staff Gen. Lawrence Welch on down, declining opposition to end its most glamorous manned-aircraft mission, but it also was discouraging congressional attempts to revive it. Never in its history had the Air Force—owned and operat-

ed by the pilot community—walked away from a manned mission, however mundane, without a fight.

The money was also an issue; $300 million is a lot to most of us, but it is chickenfeed to the Pentagon. Specifically, it is well under 7 percent of what the Pentagon spends each year on reconnaissance satellites. If the SR-71s served no other purpose than that of an emergency backup, in case of an unlucky string of satellite and launcher failures, they would be cheap insurance.

The missing piece in this puzzle, and a number of others, is a spyplane called Aurora. The outside world uses that name because a censor's slip let it appear below the SR-71 and the U-2 in the 1985 Pentagon budget request, attached to a budget line that called for production funds in 1987. Even if that was the project's real name—which is not certain—it was almost certainly changed after being compromised in such a manner.

The plane's real name has been kept secret, and so is the fact that it exists. The project is what is technical-

4

ly known as an unacknowledged Special Access Program (SAP). More often, such projects are called "black programs."

The Pentagon's "black world," within which such programs are conducted, is not a separate, secret military force. It is more like a loose underground network, distributed throughout the services and other Pentagon agencies. Its size can be gauged from the Pentagon's unclassi-

In March 1990, the the US Air Force formally retired the SR-71, allegedly abandoning a high-priority manned-aircraft mission and its fastest, highest-flying aircraft in favor of satellites. Two years later, the chief of the USAF's Space Command— charged with launching and operating those satellites—publicly confirmed that his command was, in 1990, incapable of performing its mission. Lockheed

During the first 15 years of the SR-71's career, these CIA-owned Lockheed A-12s were not officially acknowledged to exist and were protected by an active disinformation program. This did not fool the So- *viets, who knew about the program in 1960 (according to MiG bureau chief Rostislav Belyakov, in a 1991 book) and designed the MiG-25 Foxbat to intercept the A-12. Lockheed*

fied budget documents, which include correct total and summary figures but which conceal individual programs by mentioning them only by codename or by lumping them together under generic, meaningless titles.

In the Pentagon's budget request for fiscal year 1993, the black budget—expenditures masked in this way—amounted to a staggering $16 billion for research, development, and production of secret programs. That constitutes 17 percent of the Pentagon's entire budget for R&D and production, and exceeds those budgets of most Western nations.

To see the black world in action, you can trek through the Nevada desert to a mountainside overlooking the dry Groom Lake. From several miles away—as close as you can get without entering restricted government lands—you can see through the persistent haze a large flight-test center. It resembles Edwards Air Force Base, California, with a sprawling collection of hangars of many different sizes and styles, scattered by the edge of a six-mile runway.

Officially, the Groom Lake complex—also known as Area 51—does not exist. Even a Lockheed paper published last year on the early days of the U-2, which refers to tests at Groom that were completed thirty-five years ago, can describe it only as "a remote location."

Comparing today's Groom Lake with ground-level photos taken in the late 1970s, it is apparent that many of the largest buildings were added in the following decade. The site is very active: always visible in recent photos are a flotilla of Boeing 737s that bring people to Groom from the places where they live, and where their friends and families think they work—such as Palmdale, Burbank, or Edwards in California, or Nellis Air Force Base in Nevada.

The cost and inconvenience of such an operation is immense, and there is only one possible reason for it: to provide a secret testing place for aircraft that are obviously different from those the public is aware of.

Groom Lake has another unusual feature: a lake-bed runway that is six miles long, or twice as long as the longest normal runways in the United States. Going back to the basics, the length of a runway is determined either by the distance an aircraft requires to accelerate to flying speed, or the distance that the aircraft needs to decelerate after landing. That distance is proportional to the speed at which liftoff takes place; usually, ultra-long runways mean aircraft with very high minimum flying speeds, and—as is the case at Edwards—these are usually aircraft that are optimized for very high maximum speeds.

But the Air Force denies that Aurora, or any high-speed project, is among the secrets that it hides in the Nevada desert. Questioned about Aurora in the fall of 1992, former US Air Force Secretary Donald B. Rice cast doubt on "the kind of descriptions laid out in some of those articles [which] would take an aircraft of such proportions and capabilities that there wouldn't be a snowball's chance in you know where of hiding it."

Maybe, but the Air Force has done it before.

Air Force security cut its teeth on the Lockheed U-2 spyplane, the first US aircraft to be kept secret at the time it entered service. There were, however, some problems. The U-2 used daylight cameras and therefore operated in the daytime. In its original form, it could not be refueled in flight, and had to be based in allied nations on the periphery of the Soviet Union in order to reach its targets. Worst of all, it had the least intelligent cover designation in history.

The U-2 attracted attention from the moment it arrived at Royal Air Force (RAF) Lakenheath in England. In an uncanny foreshadowing of the Aurora story, a sketch of "the mysterious stranger" made by a British spotter appeared in the London-based magazine *Flight*.

The USAF finally acknowledged that the aircraft was a Lockheed U-2, and released pictures of one of the models in fake National Advisory Committee for Aeronautics (NACA) markings to bolster the story that it was engaged in high-altitude atmospheric research. But it did not take much intelligence to wonder why such an aircraft should be kept secret, or

7

why it should have a designation in the Utility category—previously used for the chunky, 200 mile per hour (mph) de Havilland Canada Otter transport.

Security did a better job next time. The U-2's intended replacement was Lockheed's giant CL-400, codenamed Suntan. The Mach 2.5 aircraft was powered by totally new air-turbo-ram-jet (ATR) engines burning liquid hydrogen. Pratt & Whitney carved a completely new facility out of the Florida Everglades to build and test the engine, and Lockheed virtually completed the first four aircraft before Suntan was canceled due to technical snags in 1958.

Not one word leaked out about Suntan until twenty years later, when Lockheed started talking about liquid hydrogen as a future aircraft fuel.

Suntan, which had been sponsored by the USAF, was replaced by a Central Intelligence Agency (CIA) project for a kerosene-fueled Mach 3 aircraft, called Gusto. After Lockheed was selected to build the aircraft, in September 1959, Gusto was renamed Oxcart.

Lockheed's initial design was called the A-11, and featured a pencil-slim forward fuselage. As design work progressed, the drawings were modified to reduce radar reflectivity: in particular, broad chines were added to the fuselage. With these changes, the aircraft that flew in April 1962 was called the A-12.

Secrecy was paramount, and Groom Lake—which had been temporarily abandoned after the U-2 was declassified—was rebuilt into a fully equipped base that would support not only the A-12 flight-tests but also the CIA's twelve operational aircraft. The A-12 was designed to be inherently more secure than the U-2 because it

could refuel in flight and was therefore much less restricted in its use of bases.

There were some close calls. On an early test flight, an A-12 was refueling from a tanker when a commercial jet cruised by, only a few thousand feet away. Government officials met the flight when it landed, briefly detained the passengers, and warned them to say nothing about anything they might have seen. On another occasion, a couple in a light aircraft got lost and landed at the first suitable field—which happened to be Groom Lake. "We scared the hell out of them and sent them on their way," recalls a former Lockheed engineer.

In May 1963, one of the A-12s crashed near Wendover, Utah. The wreckage was cleaned up, witnesses were asked to sign security agreements, and the press was told that an F-105 had crashed.

Nevertheless, the plane's existence was an almost complete surprise when President Lyndon Johnson announced its existence in February 1964. The news sparked off a flurry of speculation, but many years passed before it was realized that Johnson's statement was—to use the elegant expression once used in court by a British civil servant—"economical with the truth."

Johnson called the plane the A-11, although the A-11 had never been built, and said that "the A-11 aircraft now at Edwards AFB are undergoing extensive tests to determine their capabilities as long-range interceptors."

In fact, the USAF had ordered a development of the A-12, called the YF-12, as an interceptor, and two of them were undergoing tests at Groom. But there were no A-11s, or A-12s, or YF-12s at Edwards and never had been. In order to keep the verifiable facts consistent with the president's

While Americans were not told about the A-12, they were told about this aircraft, originally and incorrectly called an "A-11." Actually, it is a YF-12A, with national markings, buzz numbers and a fake porthole (to persuade analysts that it was a three-seater) hastily added for its first publicity shots. Lockheed

statement, the YF-12s were rushed to Edwards and—since the plan view of the aircraft was still secret—immediately placed into hangars. They were still so hot from their supersonic dash that they triggered the sprinklers in the hangar, drenching the reception committee.

The Air Force had also ordered thirty examples of the RS-71, a reconnaissance-strike airplane, developed from the YF-12, designed to assess damage after a nuclear attack and to destroy with nuclear weapons any targets that had escaped the first attack. In December 1964, Johnson revealed the existence of the aircraft, but called it the SR-71 Blackbird. Allegedly, it was a misreading, but the official designation of the aircraft was changed to SR (strategic reconnaissance) and the fact that the aircraft could have been developed easily to carry weapons was not alluded to until the early 1980s.

But the CIA's A-12s remained secret, despite the fact that by 1965 there were 1,800 people working at Groom Lake. By the end of that year

the aircraft was declared ready for operation. In May 1967, A-12s were deployed to Kadena Air Base, in Okinawa, to conduct regular flights over North Vietnam and some over North Korea. They continued to do so until mid-1968, when the CIA A-12 unit was deactivated, the aircraft were placed in secure storage at Palmdale, and the mission was assumed—for reasons of economy—by the USAF's SR-71s.

Although the A-12s had been flying regularly out of Kadena, their existence went unnoticed. So did that of a companion program to the A-12.

This was the D-21 ramjet-powered reconnaissance drone, designed to be launched at Mach 3 from the back of an A-12, and with the almost unbelievable range of more than 10,000 miles at Mach 3.8. The D-21 became operational in 1970, but was retired in 1972 for political and technical reasons after $2 billion had been spent.

A few years later, some of the D-21s were photographed in open storage at Davis-Monthan AFB, Arizona,

9

but the Air Force released scant details of them and implied that they were developed as test vehicles or target drones. The D-21s were later placed in a secure area, and their existence went unreported outside the trade press.

The A-12s were kept indoors at Palmdale, California, for ten years. The USAF had lost several SR-71s in the early years of the program, and it was felt that the A-12s might be needed as spares. In April 1982, twenty years after the first flight, the existence of the A-12 was declassified. The D-21 was revealed at the same time, but nothing was said about its capabilities, and its development history is still officially classified.

Before April 1982, the existence of the A-12 had been intentionally concealed for twenty-three years, despite flying operational missions out of non-secure bases, through a combination of security, cover stories, and misleading information. The ultimate irony is that the security measures had little effect on their intended target. The Soviet Union's intelligence services were well aware that the A-12 existed as early as 1960, MiG chief designer Belyakov revealed in a 1991 book; the MiG-25 Mach 3 fighter was designed to counter the A-12, not—as CIA leaks suggested in the late 1970s—the already moribund XB-70.

And now, it is Aurora that does not exist.

More than a dozen A-12s—as big as a B-58 bomber—were completed in total secrecy before the program's existence was acknowledged. via Jim Goodall

Chapter 1

Blackest of the Black

Surely you have heard of it?...
It has been the most jealously guarded
of all government secrets.

—Conan Doyle, *The Bruce-Partington Plans*

About a year and a half after the SR-71 was retired, around 7am on a Thursday morning in June 1991, a sonic boom rolled across the southern California basin. It was enough of a shock to make people call their local radio stations, asking if the noise had been caused by an earthquake; but it had not.

The boom was an unusual occurrence because military pilots know that booming urban areas is bad for public relations. It was also unusual in that it could be tracked and measured in a way that would be impossible anywhere else in the world: Looking for signs of the Big One—the next massive release of the tension locked in the San Andreas fault—is not only a California obsession, but a full-time job for US Geological Service (USGS) seismologists based at the California Institute of Technology in Pasadena.

The CalTech seismologists monitor and map every quiver in the ground with an array of 220 plus remote seismographs scattered across the Southland, from the southern coasts to the eastern Mojave Desert.

During the 1980s, they had found that their instruments would respond when the space shuttle orbiters passed overhead at supersonic speed, on their gliding approach to Edwards AFB. They also realized that they could reconstruct the shuttle's track and speed by comparing the time at which the boom, sweeping along like a vast cone trailed by the spacecraft, arrived at different points.

It seemed to the USGS seismologists that the June 1991 boom, and other booms that were tracked between October 1991 and June 1992, were produced by something moving between Mach 3 (2,000mph) and Mach 4 (2,650mph). The shuttle flies much faster than this during re-entry, but no shuttles were landing on those dates. The world's air speed record is 2,193mph, or Mach 3.3—set in July 1976 by the now-retired SR-71.

The track that the seismologists plotted on the map ran roughly northeast over Los Angeles and across the Mojave Desert, headed somewhere between Death Valley and Las Vegas. It pointed toward the sprawling Nellis range, the largest expanse of military testing and practice range in the Western world.

The unidentified vehicles that boomed Los Angeles in 1991 and 1992 were not heard from again beyond Nevada. In all probability, they were headed for Groom Lake. But if they *were* headed for Groom, some 300 miles from Los Angeles, they were at

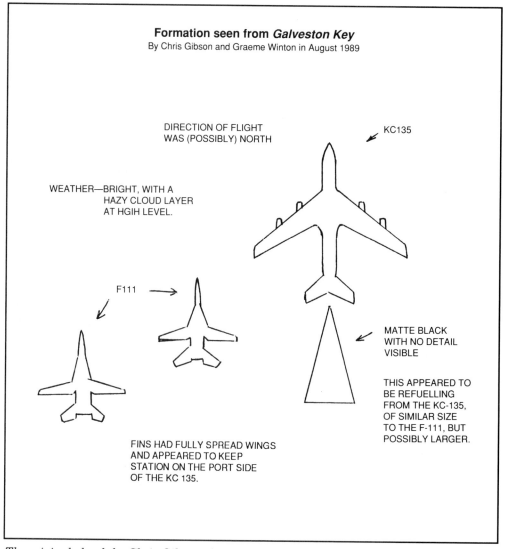

Formation seen from *Galveston Key*
By Chris Gibson and Graeme Winton in August 1989

DIRECTION OF FLIGHT
WAS (POSSIBLY) NORTH

KC135

WEATHER—BRIGHT, WITH A
HAZY CLOUD LAYER
AT HGIH LEVEL.

F111

MATTE BLACK
WITH NO DETAIL
VISIBLE

THIS APPEARED TO
BE REFUELLING
FROM THE KC-135,
OF SIMILAR SIZE
TO THE F-111, BUT
POSSIBLY LARGER.

FINS HAD FULLY SPREAD WINGS
AND APPEARED TO KEEP
STATION ON THE PORT SIDE
OF THE KC 135.

The original sketch by Chris Gibson of the aircraft which he saw over the North Sea in August 1989. Chris Gibson

most fifteen minutes from arrival. Even at their record-breaking speed, they were already decelerating.

The Los Angeles booms were more than an isolated incident. They were the first corroborated, non-hearsay evidence to support rumors, sightings, and hearings that had been accumulating since the mid-1980s.

The first reports were heard in 1986, not long after the federal government sealed off another large tract of open land near Groom Lake. The effect was to make Groom less visible to observers on public land; clearly, for some reason, the Pentagon felt that the base's security was inadequate, or was about to become so.

In February 1988, the *New York Times* reported that the USAF was working on a stealthy reconnaissance aircraft capable of Mach 6 (about 4,000mph). The story was attributed to "Pentagon sources"; other papers that tried to follow it found closed doors and a cold trail.

Early in 1990, around the time the SR-71 was retired, *Aviation Week* made another reference to such an aircraft, reporting that witnesses had heard an incredibly loud aircraft departing from Edwards at night. One of them likened the noise to "the sky being ripped open." Others referred to a "pulsing" sound that rose and fell in volume at about one cycle per second. One of the magazine's readers, responding to the story, reported seeing an aircraft traverse an estimated 400 mile distance in six minutes over the Pacific.

In November 1991, a Royal Air Force air traffic controller saw a radar blip emerge from the base at Machrihanish, Scotland, and was startled to see it accelerate to Mach 3. According to the respected Scottish daily paper *The Scotsman,* which reported the incident in February 1992, the controller called Machrihanish to ask what had transpired, and was told to forget what he had seen.

About the same time, another witness a few miles from Machrihanish reported hearing a tremendous noise, like standing directly underneath a departing military aircraft.

Machrihanish is one of the most remote, least accessible air bases in Europe. Located near the tip of the rugged Kintyre Peninsula in western Scotland, it is many hours from any large town by road, and it lies on the edge of the open Atlantic channel between Scotland and northern Ireland.

Machrihanish is usually a quiet base, used as a jumping-off point for heavily loaded C-5s and for maritime reconnaissance aircraft on North Atlantic patrols. In 1986, reports had linked Machrihanish to the then-secret F-117 stealth fighter; the base also hosts a detachment of US Navy SEAL (Sea-Air-Land) special-operations forces.

Another unexplained phenomenon was recorded in May 1992, when a photographer snapped mysterious contrails over Amarillo, Texas. Dubbed "doughnuts on a rope," the contrails appeared to emanate from a high-speed aircraft. Days later, another report of similar trails was heard; again, from the vicinity of Machrihanish.

In the fall of 1992, I received a letter from Chris Gibson, a Scottish oil-exploration engineer and a former member of the British Royal Observer Corps (ROC). The ROC was a volunteer organization that had been formed in the 1920s to identify and count enemy aircraft over Britain. It was one of the first organizations any-

13

In the late 1970s, the Soviet Union deployed this formidable SAM system, the PMU-300 (known to the West as the SA-10 Grumble). Combining long range with a sophisticated guidance suite and great mobility, it represented a serious threat to the SR-71.

where to develop ways of training and testing aircraft recognition. In the 1980s, Gibson was a master of this art, competing in international recognition tournaments where a long-distance shot of an aircraft would be flashed on a screen for a fraction of a second.

Attached to Gibson's letter was a neat, economical sketch of what he had seen from the oil rig *Galveston Key* in August 1989. Gibson had made the sketch just after the sighting, but had kept quiet about it. He was still a member of the ROC at the time, and as such had signed Britain's draconian Official Secrets Act, an evil monster of a law that had been rammed through Parliament during a 1911 German spy scare. By 1992, out of the ROC, he felt more able to reveal a drawing that had nothing to do with his ROC duties.

Gibson's rig was in the North Sea's Indefatigable field, directly beneath a twenty-by-sixty-mile block of sky called Air-to-Air Refueling Area (AARA) 6A. On that day in 1989, cruising northward through AARA 6A, were two F-111s and a KC-135 tanker—and, apparently refueling from the tanker, an airplane in the shape of a pure isoceles triangle, with a leading-edge sweep of seventy-five degrees. It was a little longer, overall, than the F-111s.

It was Aurora—or at least, what we call Aurora.

The North Sea sighting, the boom reports, and the retirement of the SR-71 suggest that Aurora was operational by mid-1989. Such aircraft are not created overnight: Aurora, with its record-shattering speed and altitude performance and its radical design, must have been flown in 1985 or 1986, and the program would have started in 1982 at the latest.

The idea that the Pentagon is still building billion-dollar aircraft in wartime-like secrecy, even after the collapse of the Soviet Union, has made skeptics out of many people. In the 1980s, the Pentagon spent billions to develop stealth aircraft that would evade defenses by being hard to detect and even more difficult to track. Why, then, should it simultaneously spend more money on hypersonic aircraft?

The answers may lie in the sweeping changes in defense policy that took place in the early 1980s—often in such secrecy that their magnitude was never fully appreciated at the time. The new administration of President Ronald Reagan, taking office in January 1981, found that there was a technology base for a hypersonic aircraft.

There were also a number of reasons why Reagan's team may have felt that there was a pressing need for such a vehicle.

By 1981, the SR-71 fleet had performed thousands of operational missions over China, North Vietnam, and the Middle East, and routinely skirted the edges of the Soviet Union—never quite breaching Eisenhower's ban on overflights but constantly irritating the Soviet air defenses. More than 800 missiles had been fired at them and no SR-71 had ever been scratched (although a missile fragment was once found lodged in one of the CIA's A-12s).

Newer missiles might pose more of a threat. In an interview in early 1983, Lockheed Skunk Works chief Ben Rich commented that the only operational system that was considered a threat to the SR-71 was the Soviet S-200 Volga surface-to-air missile (SAM), which had been specifically designed to shoot it down. Even then, it was only a threat if it was armed with a nuclear warhead: the problem was not that it could not reach the SR-71, but that it was insufficiently responsive to get close to an evading target.

The 1980s saw the advent of two new weapons, the PMU-300 (SA-10 Grumble) and the SA-12 Gladiator/Giant. Both systems have a similar maximum altitude capability to the S-200 (about 100,000 feet) but have much better tracking and guidance systems; the PMU-300, in particular, uses the same guidance principle as the US Patriot missile.

Furthermore, as the SA-10 entered service, the Soviet Union released the older SA-5 for export, supplying the weapon to Syria, Libya, and North Korea, and located sites in War-

The SA-12 Gladiator/Giant SAM system launches two different missiles. This vehicle carries the larger of them, the biggest SAM designed since the early 1960s. JDW/Charles Bickers

saw Pact territory. These developments would inhibit SR-71 operations to an increasing extent.

An aircraft that flew much faster and much higher than an SR-71 would outfly the envelope of existing missiles. Indeed, it would be very hard to design any practical missile to challenge it. A hypersonic aircraft is much harder to shoot down than is a ballistic missile. The missile is faster, but it

climbs so high on its ballistic track that the defenses get more warning of its arrival and can predict its track with greater accuracy. A missile is also unmaneuverable and, in most cases, dumb: it has no means of detecting or evading a shoot-down.

A hypersonic aircraft will not be very maneuverable in the classic sense, but it is so fast that even a gentle turn or a relatively small change in speed will put it miles away, in mere tens of seconds, from the projected interception point that the SAM used for its first fire solution.

In the thin air above 100,000 feet, a SAM would either need large control surfaces or a ramjet with thrust-vectoring control to match its target's maneuvers. It also needs a large warhead because the thin air also reduced blast effects. The result is a large, rather high drag missile—and lofting such a vehicle twenty-plus miles straight up will take a very large booster.

Finally, such a missile—even if it could be built—would be barely mobile, would probably not even protect its launch site from observation (because the range of oblique reconnaissance sensors would exceed any feasible slant range), and would be useless against low-flying targets.

Hypersonics, therefore, are not only survivable but robust: It costs substantially more to defend against them than to build them because defenses can protect only a point, while the hypersonic aircraft can be anywhere.

The age of the SR-71 fleet may also have affected the timing of the program. The Blackbirds were undergoing a major upgrade in 1981, including the installation of a completely new automatic flight and inlet control system that promised to make the aircraft considerably more reliable and safer. But it was also clear that the aircraft would need continued work to keep them maintainable in the future, partly because they used so many unique systems and components. At some point, they would have to be either substantially upgraded or replaced; otherwise, their mission would be abandoned, leaving satellites to perform US reconnaissance in defended areas.

Total reliance on satellites leaves holes in the US intelligence structure, even in the post-Cold War era. From the perspective of the new Reagan administration, in 1981, the holes would have seemed more like yawning chasms. The reasons why are rooted in the natural limitations of satellites, their checkered development history, and the Reagan team's own passionately held views of the nature of the Cold War.

When the SR-71s were retired, some reporters were told that the Blackbird had been replaced by reconnaissance satellites. They were not told this on the record, however, because, officially, there are no reconnaissance satellites. If a USAF rocket (or, until late 1992, the shuttle) launches a reconnaissance satellite, it is described as a "classified payload." However, enough is known about the development of reconnaissance satellites to give a thumbnail sketch of their capabilities, and compare their operational advantages and limitations with those of an aircraft.

The USAF provides the systems that collect two of the most important groups of foreign intelligence: signals intelligence (SIGINT) and image intelligence (IMINT). Overall responsibility for SIGINT—the interception and analysis of radio-frequency emissions from foreign military sources—rests with the National Security Agency (NSA). Where NSA devices go into space or fly, the USAF provides the platforms. The collection of image intelligence, which may be acquired by optical, infrared, or radar sensors, is coordinated by the National Reconnaissance Office (NRO).

The NSA and the NRO each spend more money than the Central Intelligence Agency (CIA). While the latter is a household word, few Americans realize that the NRO and NSA exist. This is no accident: Until the summer of 1992, it was a technical felony to reveal the existence of the NRO.

The NRO operates reconnaissance satellites of two main types: the KH-11 optical satellite, built by TRW, and the Lacrosse radar satellite, built by Martin-Marietta. Both types are launched by Titan IV rockets into polar orbits, so that they orbit at near-right-angles to the rotation of the earth. As they orbit, the earth rotates slowly beneath them, so that their orbital tracks cross the earth's entire surface.

Most targets of interest are north of the equator, so a satellite is usually launched into an elliptical orbit with its northern perigee (closest point to the earth) located over the latitudes of greatest concern. The lowest practical perigee altitude—before atmospheric drag shortens the satellite's lifetime—is some 120 miles.

When the CIA's A-12 spyplanes were being built, satellites were in their infancy. Their cameras could not match the resolution of airborne cameras, and the only way to return imagery was to use a "bucket," a jettisonable film pod. Both of these disadvantages have been overcome, by digital data transmission and better optics, but at a price.

17

The only way to take high-resolution pictures from orbital altitudes, covering points that may be hundreds of miles from the satellite's ground track, is to use the largest and most advanced telephoto lens ever created. The optical system of an imaging satellite is similar in size to a large astronomical telescope, with a primary mirror that may be more than six feet in diameter. It is mainly for this reason that optical reconnaissance satellites are very large and expensive.

Cameras on an aircraft do not have to look so far, so a much smaller camera can achieve similar resolution. The technical objective cameras fitted to the SR-71, which were installed in the chine bays, have similar resolution to the giant lenses of the KH-11.

Less is known about radar reconnaissance satellites, but they are also large and costly because their radar systems are designed to achieve high resolution at long range. Another problem is providing power for the radar. Solar cells can provide electrical power in daylight, although not on an abundant scale. They cannot help when the satellite is in the shadow of the earth—and observing targets at night is one of the main reasons for having a radar satellite in the first place. One expert has speculated that much of the Lacrosse's mass is accounted for by batteries.

The power available to energize a radar on board an aircraft, on the other hand, is limited only by the size of the generators installed; the aircraft radar needs less power in the first place because its targets are closer.

Satellite costs are concealed within the Pentagon's classified budget, but most authorities believe that each satellite costs several hundred million dollars to build and test. In addition,

each satellite is launched by a $200 million-plus rocket.

Satellites cannot be economically recovered or maintained on orbit. They require a supply of fuel to keep them in a stable orbit, and when that fuel is exhausted they are de-orbited and burn up in the atmosphere. However, the fuel is also used to change the satellite's orbit. This takes the form of an "in-plane maneuver—nudging the satellite sideways around the earth, while it continues its polar orbit.

Satellites have unique operational advantages. Once orbited, they provide routine and consistent coverage over large areas. They cannot be shot down, and their operations, by international law, are not a violation of another country's sovereignty.

On the other hand, satellites are predictable. They can be observed as they are launched, and tracked with telescopes and radar, and their rising and setting times can be accurately predicted. This allows intelligence targets to conceal or mask their activities. A satellite operator can surprise the target once with an in-plane maneuver, but every such maneuver eats into the satellite's fuel reserve and hence its life expectancy.

An aircraft is more unpredictable. It can be made even more so if its operational tempo and routines are concealed by basing it in an area where its departure cannot be observed by foreign agents. Time-over-target is controlled by the operator: a pass may be selected to coincide with a specific event (ships leaving port at high tide, for instance), to take advantage of low, direct morning or evening light, or to catch a predicted break in the weather.

Longevity is another advantage of the aircraft. Not all satellites are maneuvered in the same way over their lifetimes, which accounts for differences in life expectancy among satellites. So far, the longest survival time for any reconnaissance satellite is five years, for a KH-11 launched in 1987. However, analysts suspect that the craft had been inoperative before it was de-orbited in 1992. Three years is a more typical lifetime. Each satellite on orbit, therefore, represents a $200 million-plus annual amortized cost for hardware alone.

The SR-71s had been in service for more than twenty-one years when they were retired. Even if a replacement aircraft cost a billion dollars, the hardware portion of its total life-cycle cost would be one-third to one-quarter of the cost of keeping one satellite station filled over the same period.

Another disadvantage of satellites is that it is hard to balance peacetime needs with wartime or crisis demands. In peacetime, it hardly matters if a target is covered by cloud today: another satellite pass will get it tomorrow or the day after. This cuts no ice with a combat commander who needs to know if his aircraft must re-attack a target within hours, or a commander-in-chief who needs to know if an invasion threat to an ally is real or a bluff.

One way to increase the frequency of passes is to orbit more satellites during a crisis. But this demands a large reserve stock of satellites and rockets, something which can be done with small, low-resolution vehicles but not with the big, expensive satellites in use now. The other way to increase the number of passes is to make extravagant use of in-plane maneuvers, but this may result in a lack of coverage later, as satellites run out of fuel ahead of schedule, and before replace-

Spectacular at launch, massive in its lifting capacity, the Space Shuttle has proven disappointing in its military utility. Once seen as the exclusive launcher of US military satellites, the Shuttle flew its last Pentagon mission in late 1992. Rockwell

ment vehicles can be completed, tested, and put on orbit.

Satellite management was at the root of the controversy over satellite coverage in the Gulf. At a postwar conference, retired USAF chief of staff Gen. Michael Dugan commented that satellites had failed to support the combat units "because they were scheduled by God and Kepler." Bernard Randolph, a former commander of USAF's Space Systems Division

19

Developed by LTV, the ASM-135 anti-satellite (ASAT) system carried under this F-15 proved capable of destroying satellites in orbit with a shotgun blast of metal fragments. LTV

and now a senior TRW executive, riposted that the satellites were "scheduled by some weenie in Washington, which is why they didn't support the troops."

Desert Storm commander Gen. Charles A. Horner, commander-in-chief of the US Space Command, pointed out that "in the black world, the customer, the operator and the acquirer are all the same [that is, the NRO] and I am not sure that serves the black world well, because certainly we found in Desert Storm that the customer happened to be operating out of the Middle East."

Aircraft are far more flexible as well. Assuming that satellites are the most cost-effective means of handling the bulk of peacetime reconnaissance, a wing of spyplanes might fly only a handful of operational missions in a month, plus a few more sorties for training, but most training could be carried out on a simulator. In a crisis, however, aircraft can shift to a higher operational tempo or even "surge" for a short period, flying ten or more times as many sorties as in peacetime.

Adding more satellites, too, provides better coverage over the entire world; extra aircraft missions are directed only where they are needed.

The satellite's basic drawbacks have always been appreciated. In fact, in the 1970s, a serious attempt was made to overcome them. Many of the reconnaissance satellite's disadvantages would be much less important if it was practical to refuel or repair the satellite on orbit, or to bring it down to earth, refurbish it, and send it up again. The NRO planned to do exactly this in the early 1970s, using the space shuttle.

From its inception, the shuttle was an amphibian, living mostly in the glaring light of the National Aeronautics and Space Administration's (NASA) publicity machine but drawing much of its nourishment from the black depths of the intelligence community.

When NASA began to study the shuttle in the late 1960s, the agency saw that the project could not make economic sense unless the shuttle replaced all other US space launchers, including those which the USAF used to launch the NRO's spy satellites. The Department of Defense (DoD) agreed to this before the shuttle program started in July 1972.

In 1972, a shuttle flight was supposed to cost $10.5 million, and four orbiters were expected to make 580 flights between 1979 and 1990, or about 50 flights per year. About a dozen flights a year would start at Space Launch Complex 6 at Vandenberg Air Force Base, Lompoc, California, from which the satellites could be safely launched into polar orbits.

Shuttle flights would be so frequent and cheap that the NRO could plan a new class of long-lived, refue-

lable, recoverable satellites. This became the Lockheed Missiles and Space Company KH-12—an extremely capable, multi-spectral imaging satellite which, because it could be refueled, would have an almost unlimited maneuvering capability. It would also have some surge capacity: In a crisis, the NRO could drive the KH-12s all over the map and bump other payloads from the shuttle manifest to make way for more refueling flights.

The shuttle fell light years short of NASA's predictions, however. *Columbia* made its first flight in April 1981, two years behind schedule; it was clear by then that the shuttle's frequency and cost goals would not be attained. A 1980 manifest called for thirty-nine flights by September 1984; by the time that date arrived, however, only twelve flights had been performed. There were also serious technical problems with the Vandenberg facility. In view of the delays, the USAF prevailed on the DoD to abandon its commitment to use the shuttle exclusively, and ordered a new generation of Titan boosters from Martin-Marietta.

Then, on the twenty-fifth shuttle flight in January 1986, the orbiter *Challenger* exploded. Soon afterward, the USAF mothballed the Vandenberg facility. A modified KH-12, to be launched by the new Titan, was under consideration for some time but appears to have been abandoned in 1988.

But the operational potential of the KH-12 had begun to diminish long before it was canceled. Every time the shuttle schedule slipped or the cost of a shuttle launch went up, the KH-12 became less flexible and less economical.

The *Challenger* loss was also a reminder that an air-breathing reconnaissance system is an accident-insurance policy. In 1985 and 1986, as the NRO was planning to phase out the KH-11 in favor of the KH-12, the loss of the *Challenger* and the explosions of two Titan boosters left the United States with only one IMINT satellite in orbit. Even in 1992, according to General Horner, DoD launches were chronically late, and the limitations of launch facilities have put the schedule "in a hole that we cannot get out of."

By 1981, nobody could realistically assert that a shuttle-supported satellite could match the flexibility, longevity, and surge capability of the aircraft at any reasonable cost; one more argument against an SR-71 replacement was on the point of collapse.

But there was another, much more important reason why it is most unlikely that the Reagan administration would have neglected the need to keep a robust, air-breathing reconnaissance capability. Most discussions of the reconnaissance abilities of satellites and aircraft, including the preceding paragraphs, rest on one assumption: that both are used in peacetime or in medium-intensity Vietnam-type conflicts, in which the worst threat to the reconnaissance vehicle is a SAM fired in direct defense of hostile territory.

Reagan's strategic advisors, veterans of the ominously named Committee on the Present Danger, believed that assumptions of that kind were suicidally dangerous. They believed that the Soviet Union was arming for conventional war and seeking nuclear superiority, preparing to fight and win a nuclear war that might last weeks or months. Unless the United States developed a similar or superior capability, they believed, the country would be unable to risk the use of nuclear weapons and would be likely to lose

the initiative in any conventional conflict.

In October 1981, President Reagan signed National Security Decision Directive 13 (NSDD-13), which instructed and authorized the Pentagon to plan and equip for a six-month nuclear war ending in victory. The goal was to develop systems that could support "controlled nuclear counter-attacks over an extended period while maintaining a reserve of nuclear forces sufficient for trans- and post-attack protection and coercion."

The Pentagon began to invest hundreds of billions of dollars in new nuclear weapons, such as the B-2 bomber, the Advanced Cruise Missile, the Trident D5 submarine-launched missile, and the MX rail-mobile heavy ballistic missile. Less visible but just as important was the Milstar communications satellite system, designed to maintain control over this new force.

All the new weapons had two features in common: they were designed to ride out a first-strike nuclear attack, and they were accurate and could be easily retargeted. Milstar was the nuclear machine's nervous system, sending targeting data to the platforms. But it would all be much less useful if the system was blind.

There is no sign that the NRO's reconnaissance satellite system was ever designed to survive a nuclear war. It could barely endure a conventional conflict. Moreover, the balance of power in a space war was tilted in favor of the Soviet Union.

The Soviet Union had deployed an operational anti-satellite (ASAT) system in the mid-1970s, and although the effectiveness of this weapon was disputed (the Pentagon said it would work) there was no reason that a better system could not be developed, based either on missiles or on ground-based lasers.

The US did develop a small air-launched ASAT, but did not field it. ASAT technology was more dangerous to the United States—which launched relatively few, long-lived satellites—than the Soviet Union, which launched four to five times as many vehicles in an average year. The Soviet satellites were less valuable targets and easier to replace.

The US launch facilities were also far more vulnerable than their Soviet equivalents. Both US launch bases—NASA's Kennedy Space Center and the USAF's Vandenberg AFB—are coastal sites that can be kept under continuous surveillance from international airspace; both, in the kind of conventional war envisaged in the Cold War era, could have been attacked by non-nuclear, radar-guided heavy cruise missiles launched by Tu-95 long-range aircraft or submarines; both, even now, are more vulnerable than most sites to covert seaborne attack.

While the United States could be taken out of the space launch business quite quickly, the Soviet Union's launch sites were located deep inside the Soviet Union, immune from conventional attack.

What the early 1980s warfighting plans apparently lacked, and it was a glaring omission, was any sign of a survivable, controllable reconnaissance system that could find mobile targets, such as missile launchers, or assess damage to protected or fixed targets. The KH-12 could not fulfil this mission because the shuttles that would service it were not survivable.

A hypersonic aircraft, on the other hand, could fill the target-spotting role easily. Assuming that Milstar sur-

vived as designed, it could transmit reconnaissance data back to the attack control center in real time, where it could be interpreted and used as the basis for targeting. The hypersonic aircraft could search roads and rail lines for mobile intercontinental ballistic missiles (ICBM) and communications systems, and check air bases for surviving bombers.

The hypersonic aircraft could pass targeting data to ICBMs, D5s, or B-2s, and might also be teamed with more radical weapons. In the early 1980s, Lockheed Missiles and Space Company won a secret contract to develop a strategic hypersonic-glide vehicle (HGV). It was designed to be launched from a B-52, at 68,000 feet—it is seldom realized that a B-52 can reach that kind of altitude, but it can—it would be rocket-boosted to Mach 18 at high altitude, and could glide more than 5,000 miles to its target, arriving barely thirty minutes after launch. The main challenge was aerodynamic heating: the HGV was made of heat-resistant carbon-carbon composite skin panels on a titanium substructure. Its planform, interestingly enough, was a pure triangle with its leading edges swept at seventy-five degrees.

With the response speed of the ballistic missile and the short warning time and terminal maneuver performance of a cruise missile, the HGV could be launched against mobile targets detected by Aurora and hit them before they had time to move.

It is an outside chance that Aurora itself was, like the SR-71, designed for a reconnaissance-strike mission, not just spotting for other weapons. Ben Rich, in a 1983 interview, lamented the fact that the SR-71 had never been armed. He noted that the standard AGM-69 Short-Range Attack Missile, which would fit in an SR-71's chine bay, would go 30 miles from a sea-level launch, 100 miles from a B-52's cruising altitude, and 500 miles from an SR-71. "We need to make the Soviets worry about aircraft at 100,000 feet," he said. "We've given away the high ground."

Hypersonic aircraft have a unique offensive potential because they are immune from direct attack by the defenses, and because their sheer speed can be turned into a kill mechanism. McDonnell Douglas studied hypersonic strike aircraft that were armed with conical missiles that resembled ICBM re-entry vehicles. The missiles were boosted to Mach 12 after launch and were designed to hit their targets at more than Mach 7.

Unlike an aircraft, these one-shot vehicles could be protected from the heat by ablative coatings, making such high speeds possible at low altitude. They would be accurate because their launch aircraft, safe from defensive fire, could guide them all the way to impact via a microwave link; studies showed that they would hit within fifteen feet of their aim-points.

"At 6,000 feet per second, a pound of metal releases as much energy as a pound of TNT," says Paul Czysz, professor of aerospace engineering at St Louis University and one of the leading US experts on hypersonic technology, who worked on some of the McDonnell studies. A solid penetrator weighing 200 pounds would "carry enough energy to lift the *Kirov* [a 28,000 ton Soviet cruiser] ten feet out of the water," he explains. However, what it would actually do is slice through the ship's steel sides like a hot knife through butter.

Alternatively, an explosive cord could peel open the penetrator body just before impact and dispense a hail of tungsten darts called flechettes. Three-pound flechettes would shred a concrete bridge and one-pound darts would destroy tanks.

Hypersonics could also play a role in the emerging doctrine of "nonlethal warfare," which looks at ways of disabling or destroying the machines of war without killing their operators. For example, a 100 pound payload of BB-size pellets, dispensed into a 100 foot diameter cloud, would obliterate every radar and communications antenna on a warship and leave it blind and deaf, without sinking it or harming any crew below deck. It is more likely, though, that Aurora was designed as an intelligence-gathering system because this would explain the secrecy that has enshrouded the program from birth.

For the national-intelligence community—the CIA, NSA, and NRO, and all the activities that relate to their missions—to deliberately deceive the public is not just an unfortunate necessity. Cover and covert are the principal words in the secret world's vocabulary. "As open war depends on weapons, so does the secret war depend on cover," a former CIA operative explained in the 1963 book *A Short Course in the Secret War* by James McCarga. "Weapons are not in themselves the purpose of war, but they shield the soldier and enable him to advance to his objective—or they protect his retreat. Cover shields the secret agent from his opposition."

The community has shielded its technical means of gathering intelligence as tightly as it has shielded its human agents. If an adversary knows next to nothing about the systems that can observe him, the argument runs, he is unable to use camouflage, con-

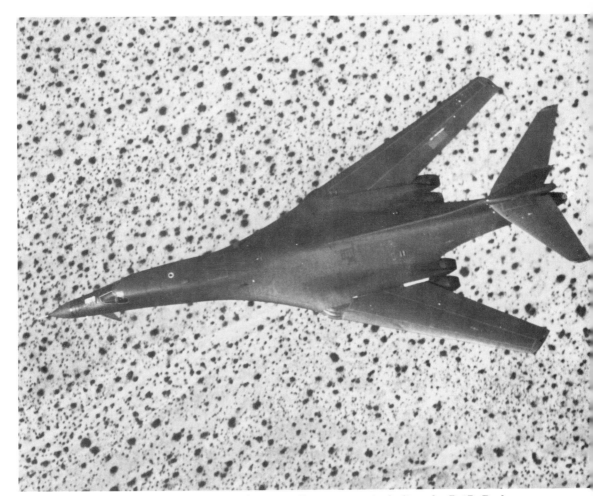

In the early 1980s, the Pentagon invested billions in new, mobile, accurate nuclear strike weapons, including the B-1B. Rockwell

cealment, and deception to frustrate or mislead the US intelligence community. Lifting the cover on intelligence systems reduces their value.

Since the US intelligence community took shape in the 1950s, it has revealed as little about its activities as possible. Officially, the US government has never launched any spy satellites; one of the reasons that we know they exist and that we know what their lifetimes are is that their launches cannot be concealed and that they can be tracked in space.

In 1991, an apparently genuine CIA history of the A-12 program was circulated widely among Skunk Works observers and insiders. One of the issues it discussed was the replacement of the A-12 by the SR-71. The author

Northrop's B-2 stealth bomber was designed to drop nuclear bombs with pinpoint accuracy on heavily protected, well-defended targets, cued by the expensive, hardened Milstar satellite system—but the satellites that would provide the data that Milstar would disseminate would quickly be destroyed in any nuclear war. Northrop noted that the CIA campaigned strongly to keep the A-12s in service, in parallel with the USAF's open SR-71 operation. One reason was that, in the CIA's view, covert was better, increasing the possibility of surprise and confusing the adversary's counterintelligence experts.

Aircraft can be more covert than satellites. As the SR-71s showed in 1973, when they flew 15,000 mile nonstop missions over the Middle East, aircraft can cover the entire globe without landing outside the United States. They are not up in space and able to be tracked twenty-four hours a day, and their takeoffs cannot be observed as satellite launches can.

In the 1980s, the secrecy that had formerly covered intelligence activities was extended to the new weapons of nuclear warfighting. The B-2 was developed as a black program, and its operational characteristics—range, bombload, and sensors—were strictly classified. Milstar was similarly classified. The Lockheed HGV project was even more deeply buried.

It is therefore not at all difficult to believe that, in 1981–1982, the US government awarded a development contract for a hypersonic manned reconnaissance aircraft to succeed the SR-71, to complement a constellation of nonrecoverable satellites in peacetime, and to provide wartime reconnaissance for nuclear warfighting weapons; and that the project was, from the start, covered by the same level of classification as reconnaissance satellites.

Lockheed's Skunk Works, now the Lockheed Advanced Development Company, is by far the most likely prime contractor for Aurora. Throughout the 1980s, financial analysts have concluded that Lockheed has been en-gaged in several very large classified projects, but they have never been able to identify enough of them to account for all the company's income.

Technically, the Skunk Works has a unique record of managing large, high-risk programs under a veil of unparalleled secrecy. It also has a record, even in such risky projects, of delivering what it promised to deliver.

With the collapse of the Soviet empire in the late 1980s, many people felt that the US government's covert activities would be cut back. This happened, but only to some extent. The black budget peaked in 1988, and declined steeply thereafter as the Pentagon declassified spending figures for major weapon systems such as the B-2 and Milstar.

The core of the black budget—most of it to do with intelligence collection—is intact. As noted earlier, the Pentagon's unclassified budget request for fiscal year 1993 appears to include almost $16 billion for classified research, development, and procurement projects.

This is only an estimate, based on the assumption that the unclassified DoD budget includes accurate total budgets for all services and most DoD agencies.

Black programs are camouflaged in several ways in the unclassified version of the budget. Some are identified by codenames. Air Force codenamed line items such as Centennial and Senior Citizen (both tactical R&D programs) have no dollar amounts listed. But individual service budgets include subtotals for different categories of spending. For example, in the case of USAF R&D on strategic systems, the total of the line items in the category does not equal the category total. The difference—$399 million—is accounted for by black programs. Research and development associated with intelligence programs is 95 percent black: $2.4 billion in fiscal year 93.

Classified funding is also concealed under umbrella line items. For instance, a single line item for "selected activities" is buried in the penultimate page of the USAF procurement budget, under "other procurement" and listed below such exciting items as "pallet, air cargo."

At $5.56 billion, it is the biggest single line item in the entire DoD equipment budget. It is four- fifths as large as the entire procurement budget for the US Army, and it has increased to match inflation since 1991.

About three-quarters of the black money (just under $12 billion) was requested for Air Force programs: $3.6 billion for research and development and $8.3 billion for procurement—production of weapons, spares, and support equipment. The main reason for this is that the activities that support intelligence-gathering systems are overwhelmingly buried within the Air Force.

There are some large uncertainties in calculations of this kind. Analyst John Pike of the Federation of American Scientists, for example, is convinced that the vast "Selected Activities" line item is in fact the operating budget of the CIA, rather than being part of USAF procurement.

On the other hand, the process of calculating the black budget from the gaps and inconsistencies in the unclassified edition seems suspiciously simple. As noted in Tim Weiner's detailed study of the black budget, *Blank Check*, the intelligence world can also be funded from other programs: unspent funds can be transferred from almost any federal activity with very little effective oversight. There is no overt evidence that intelligence activities have been supported by funds from outside the Pentagon budget, but no-one who has studied the spooks' Byzantine history would dismiss such a possibility as out of hand.

What is certain is that the black budget in the 1980s contained enough money for an Aurora program. At an educated guess, such a project would probably have cost around $1 billion a year on research and development, in its peak years, plus several hundred million dollars for each aircraft. There would probably not be many aircraft involved: the CIA built only fifteen A-12s, and less than twenty Auroras would probably fill any conceivable mission requirement. The aircraft would have been hand-built, to a great extent: Extensive tooling and automation would make no sense for a short production run.

In 1990s Pentagon argot, Aurora is what is called a "silver bullet" program: a system acquired in small numbers, but so revolutionary in its capabilities that it is virtually invulnerable and capable of influencing the outcome of a large-scale conflict even if deployed in ones and twos. The F-117 and B-2 are silver bullets; so was the SR-71.

Aurora and the reconnaissance satellite program are still kept secret, despite the end of the Cold War, because the intelligence operators like it that way. Up to the beginning of 1993, they had one of their own in the White House: George Bush was the only US president to have served as the director of Central Intelligence—the supreme commander of the CIA, NSA, and NRO.

Do not bet the rent that things will change under the new administra-

Another weapon designed for nuclear warfighting was the Midgetman small Intercontinental Ballistic Missile (ICBM), to be carried in the Hard Mobile Launcher (HML) shown here. Midgetman was de- *signed specifically to attack targets that survived a first wave of missiles, but would be of limited use without a viable reconnaissance system to support it. Boeing*

tion. The last new Democratic president came to office with a pledge to open up the government that had done so much to implement Nixon's secret and illegal commands. Jimmy Carter passed the Freedom of Information Act. He also presided over the launch of the first stealth aircraft, the biggest black-world project since the atom bomb. His right-hand man in that venture, Dr. William J. Perry, is back in Washington as deputy secretary of defense to the Clinton administration.

However, both Congress and other parts of the military are pressing for some changes in the intelligence community. In particular, reforms have been proposed that would reduce the dominance of the CIA and place the NRO under a new directorate of imaging intelligence. This would be responsible not only for supporting national foreign intelligence programs, but also, to a much greater extent, for providing reconnaissance for forces in the field.

Both satellites and air-breathers have important missions in the post-Soviet world. The Gulf War was an example: imagery that showed the massing of Iraqi forces close to the Saudi border, immediately after the invasion of Kuwait, was apparently critical in persuading Saudi Arabia's King Fahd to invite coalition forces into his country.

Nuclear and chemical weapons, long-range missiles, and other delivery systems could be critical in future regional conflicts. Embargoes and international treaties have persuaded many countries to launch their own domestic projects to develop such weapons, usually in secret. Detailed overhead imagery, with the highest possible resolution, provides hard evidence of such efforts and can reveal how far they have progressed.

In the former Soviet Union, Russia has agreed to drastic cuts in its nuclear weapons, as long as it knows that the other former republics will make good on their pledges to renounce them. High-resolution imagery can show whether a missile silo has really been destroyed, and whether all missiles in a certain location have been removed.

The people who own these intelligence targets have enough sense and technical capability to map the orbits of reconnaissance satellites. Neither are camouflage and deception expensive or high-tech activities.

The world has come to depend on its spies in the sky. Satellite and aircraft intelligence have dispelled myths and reduced fear and tension from their earliest days. Without overhead imaging reconnaissance, arms control would have been impossible. In the unstable, unpredictable future, the idea of attempting to manage or mediate a crisis on the other side of the globe without accurate, real-time image intelligence is ludicrous. It just cannot be done.

It can be argued that a combination of satellites and aircraft is a more economical approach to this task, more robust against simple countermeasures and accidental failures, than either satellites or aircraft alone. In some ways, the question is not "Why Aurora?" but "Why not earlier?

Chapter 2

Flying Toward Space

**There is a strong family resemblance about misdeeds,
and if you have the details of a thousand at your finger ends,
it is odd if you can't unravel the thousand and first.**

—Conan Doyle, *A Study in Scarlet*

In 1971, Senator Barry Goldwater became one of the first civilians to take a ride in the SR-71. The SR-71's creator, Clarence L. "Kelly" Johnson, was there to brief Goldwater. After the flight—according to SR-71 pilot Abe Kardong—Goldwater asked Johnson where the next step would be.

"Mach 6", Johnson replied.

Aurora may have been hard to develop, but it certainly would not have been impossible. In fact, many people will assert that it could, should, and would have been done a long time ago, were it not for some short-sighted, panicky decisions in the 1960s.

In the days of Elvis and the Edsel, military planners confidently believed that hypersonic fighters and bombers would be in service by the early 1970s. The first half-century in the development of practical military aircraft could be charted in terms of increasing speed—but never more so than in the years after World War II.

In the twenty years after the end of World War I, the speeds of military aircraft doubled. Although war is often considered a spur to high technology,

most military aircraft increased only a little in the war years. By 1945, only a handful of jets had broken the 500mph barrier—but it was the start of a speed explosion.

In 1960, aircraft that could exceed 1,500mph were going into squadron service. Aircraft capable of 2,000mph were under development, and were supposed to be in service by 1965: a fourfold increase in speed in about twenty years.

The next logical step was to hypersonic speeds. The definition of "hypersonic" is not quite as neat as "supersonic," but aerodynamicists consider that the hypersonic realm starts when the air in front of the vehicle's leading edges "stagnates": a band of air is trapped, unable to flow around the vehicle, and reaches extremely high pressures and temperatures. As a rule of thumb, the edge of the hypersonic regime lies at a speed of roughly a mile per second—3,600mph or Mach 5.4.

Three technology streams led toward hypersonic flight in the 1940s and 1950s. One was the development

The aggressive pursuit of speed in the post-war era is typified by the Douglas X-3. Designed in 1945, when the official world's air speed record still stood at 469 mph, the X-3 was intended for sustained flight

of an engine that could propel a vehicle at such speeds, if only for a few moments. Another was the exploration of hypersonic aerodynamics as a means of overcoming a fundamental problem of space exploration: bringing a space vehicle out of orbit in one piece. A third was the development of engines for sustained high-Mach flight.

The first breakthrough came in the late 1930s, with the development of practical rocket engines. In one of history's extraordinary feats of technology, Wernher von Braun's team succeeded—in October 1942—in launching an A-4 missile powered by a 55,000 pound-thrust liquid rocket engine, fifteen times more powerful than any other engine even conceived at that time.

Not only did the Germans develop and deploy the first ballistic missile, but they originated a different concept: the hybrid ballistic/aerodynamic or boost-glide vehicle.

The starting point for these studies was the fact that the A-4 missile struck the ground at 2,000mph; this was far more than necessary to evade any contemporary defenses, and represented wasted energy. Von Braun decided to fit wings to the A-4, so that it would descend in a high-speed glide rather than a ballistic dive. The range of the weapon would be almost doubled.

The winged missile was called the A-9. Tests in Peenemunde's Mach 4.4 shock tunnel, the only installation of its type in the world, led to the choice of small, thin, sweptback wings of very low aspect ratio. Design work was suspended in late 1943 due to problems with the basic A-4, but resumed a year later because the Allies were overrunning the territory from which A-4s could reach their intended targets. A winged test vehicle, the A-4b, attained 2,700mph in early 1945.

Also on the drawing board was a manned aircraft based on the A-9, with a retractable landing gear, flaps, and airbrakes. It was designed to achieve a maximum speed of

2,800mph in a boosted climb to 95,000 feet.

Even that proposal paled beside the visionary project of Eugen Sanger and Irene Bredt: a 100 ton rocket bomber with a global range. It would be launched from a two-mile sled track that would accelerate it to Mach 1.5. Released from the track, the bomber would climb to 5,500 feet before the rocket ignited. The bomber would then climb steeply to 130,000 feet, converting much of its 90 tons of fuel into potential and kinetic energy.

Next, the Sanger bomber would dive down into thicker air where its wings could generate more lift, and pull up into a ballistic trajectory, using most of the rest of its fuel and peaking 175 miles above the earth. It would not have enough energy to go into orbit, but that was not Sanger's intention. Instead, as it approached 130,000 feet on its dive back to earth, it would pull up into another ballistic arc,

peaking 115 miles up. The bomber would continue around the world with a series of progressively lower and shorter arcs until its energy was exhausted and it commenced a long, slow glide back to base.

After the war, the Sanger project proved highly influential in the United States. Dr. Walter Dornberger, who had been a key member of the German V-2 rocket team and who was familiar with Sanger's work, went to work for Bell Aircraft Corporation, which had assumed leadership in the development of specialized high-speed research aircraft. Dornberger managed to raise considerable interest in suborbital boost-glide concepts, descendants of the A-9, in the 1950s.

At the same time, more conventional aircraft—designed for constant speed in level flight—were pushing toward higher performance. From 1944 onward, the USAF and NACA (National Advisory Committee for Aero-

In 1945, even Mach 2 was not the limit. With a steel structure and a turbopump-fed liquid rocket, the Bell X-2—ordered in that year, but not flown at its design speed until ten years later—was aimed at Mach 3. USAF

nautics) used experimental aircraft to fly out to higher speeds and altitudes before designers put pencil to paper on practical aircraft that would operate in those regimes.

The plan had mixed success (the X-2 was less of a trailblazer than an example of how not to do Mach 3) but the objective was sound, and, from 1952–1953, similar considerations drove the USAF, NACA, and the Office of Naval Research—which had sponsored the Mach 2 Douglas D-558-2 Skyrocket —to think about a hypersonic research vehicle.

Research into ramjets and other unconventional engines for sustained flight close to Mach 3 was a priority in the 1945–1960 era. The North American Navaho supersonic cruise missile used two Curtiss-Wright ramjets in the cruise, but was lifted and accelerated by a liquid-rocket booster. USAF

In 1954, the Navy program was merged with the USAF-NACA effort. Late in the year, NACA issued a requirement for an air-launched manned research vehicle with a maximum speed of more than Mach 6 and a maximum altitude of more than fifty miles. North American Aviation Incorporated beat Douglas, Bell, and Republic Aviation Corporation, and was awarded the contract for the new research vehicle, called the X-15.

The X-15 was a rugged, simple aircraft that included everything it needed to accomplish its mission and excluded everything else. It used a conventional ejection seat and a pressure suit rather than the fashionable capsule. The seat was patterned on a tractor seat. This emphasis on simplicity was to pay off in the longest and most successful test program in the rocket series. Three X-15s flew more than 300 missions, exceeding all the speed and altitude goals set at the beginning of the program.

Very early in the game, some of the principals in the X-15 program—including North American chief designer Harrison Storms, X-15 chief engineer Charles Feltz, and chief company test pilot Scott Crossfield—conceived a follow-on effort in which a modified X-15 would be mounted on one of the boosters from the Navaho missile.

The North American XSM-64 Navaho was one of the most important programs the USAF ever canceled. The huge ramjet-powered Mach 3 missile broke a vast amount of new ground in high-speed propulsion and navigation. One of the many new technologies that it needed was a liquid-rocket booster large enough to loft it to a speed and height where its ramjets would work.

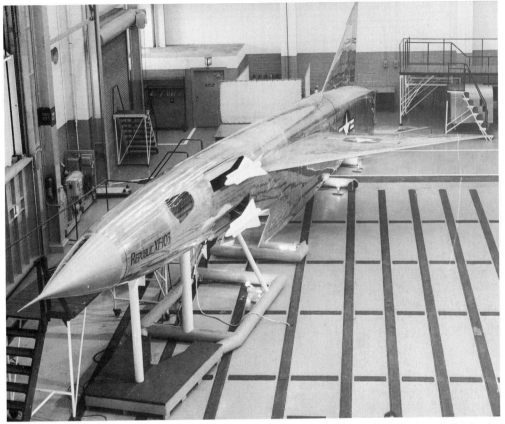

The Republic XF-103 was designed in 1950 as a Mach 3 interceptor. Its Curtiss-Wright powerplant was an "under-and-over" turbo-ramjet, with an afterburning turbojet that both accelerated the aircraft to a speed where the ramjet would ignite and brought the fighter home after its interception run. Republic via Richard De-Meis

North American formed a new division to develop the rocket motors for the three-motor, 415,000 pound-thrust booster and named it Rocketdyne. (The Navaho booster engine, the LR-105, was used in the Atlas missile and in all its subsequent space-launcher derivatives, up to the present day.)

As the initial X-15 approached its first flight, the Navaho had been canceled and several complete boosters were available. The team calculated that the X-15 could attain Mach 12 after a Navaho launch, and have a range of 9,000 miles: it did not escape their attention that it was enough to cross the Soviet Union after a launch from the United States and land at a friendly base. The only modification required to the X-15, as far as the initial studies were concerned, was some structural beefing-up to withstand the greater heat generated by the faster re-entry.

The final XF-103 configuration had an extended inlet lip and round nozzle. Republic via Richard DeMeis

After the Soviet Union put *Sputnik 1* into orbit, in October 1957, the plans grew more ambitious; the advanced X-15 became an orbital system using three Navaho boosters and a scaled-up, two-person X-15B. But there were problems. The X-15 itself was unproven and behind schedule, mainly due to delays with the Reaction Motors XLR-99 rocket engine, while the nine-engine booster seemed complex and unwieldy.

At the same time, work within Bell, Martin, Boeing, and the USAF was pointing to the boost-glide vehicle as a simpler system that would perform in roughly the same way. Starting in the mid-1950s, this work led to a series of NACA and USAF studies including Hywards (hypersonic winged research and development system); WS-118P, and Brass Bell, both

designed for reconnaissance missions; and ROBO, for rocket bomber, which was an intercontinental boost-glide missile.

In November 1957, the USAF issued a preliminary requirement for a boost-glide vehicle called Dyna-Soar—indicating that it would use both "dynamic" (orbital) and "soaring" (aerodynamic) principles to stay aloft. The basic difference between this system and the X-15B was that the propulsion and fuel tankage was removed from the orbiting and re-entry vehicle, reducing the mass that had to be protected from high temperatures. Thus, it could be launched into sub-orbital flight by a modified intercontinental ballistic missile (ICBM) like a Titan.

Dyna-Soar was a research vehicle, as originally planned, but the Air Force left little doubt that it was interested in its military potential, both as a reconnaissance platform and as a means of reaching and holding the "high ground" of space.

The value of space-based reconnaissance was clear because a spacecraft would be almost impossible to intercept. By the late 1950s, however, it was not clear how reconnaissance imagery could be returned to earth without bringing the entire satellite out of orbit.

A recoverable boost-glide vehicle promised a solution to such problems.

A manned, maneuverable spacecraft would also be able to rendezvous with Soviet satellites and examine them for evidence of reconnaissance devices and nuclear ordnance: at that time, orbital weapons had not been outlawed.

After a contest with a Bell-Martin team, Boeing was selected to build the X-20 Dyna-Soar in November 1959. The vehicle was a small, delta-wing glider, made largely of "refractory" metal alloys that tolerate high temperatures and re-radiate heat. High-nickel-content steel was to be

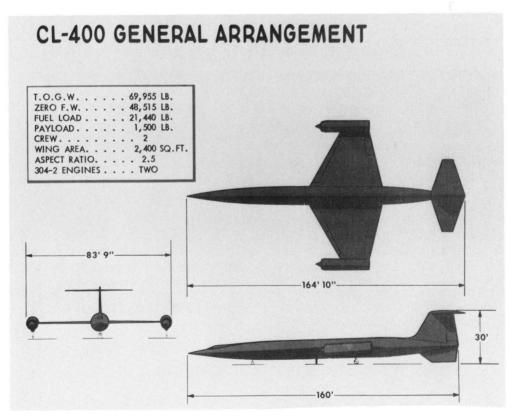

CL-400 GENERAL ARRANGEMENT

T.O.G.W.	69,955 LB.
ZERO F.W.	48,515 LB.
FUEL LOAD	21,440 LB.
PAYLOAD	1,500 LB.
CREW	2
WING AREA	2,400 SQ. FT.
ASPECT RATIO	2.5
304-2 ENGINES	TWO

83' 9"

164' 10"

30'

160'

Lockheed's CL-400, designed as a Mach 2.5 replacement for the U-2, was to be powered by Pratt & Whitney PW304 engines burning liquid hydrogen. The first exam- *ples of the huge but very light CL-400 were nearly complete when the program was canceled in 1957. Lockheed*

Designed in 1957–1960, the graceful North American XB-70 was designed to achieve high efficiency through a very close integration of propulsion and aerodynamics. The wedge-shaped body below the wing contained engines, weapons bay, and landing gear, and was shaped to generate a series of shock waves that actually increased lift and reduced drag. Rockwell

used in most of the structure, alloys based on molybdenum and columbium would be used in the leading edges, and the nose-cap, made by LTV, was ceramic.

Some design features pointed clearly to the fact that Dyna-Soar was a short step from an operational vehicle. Unlike previous re-entry systems, it had no ablative coatings, so it could be turned around quickly between flights. The USAF also made much of the fact that Dyna-Soar would be able to land at any USAF base.

Launched from the A-12 at Mach 3, the D-21 completed its entire mission in the best *operating envelope for its ramjet engine.* Lockheed

At first, the Air Force planned to start with a series of sub-orbital flights, using a Titan II booster. Orbiting flights would need more power, provided by strapping on large solid-rocket boosters to the sides of the Titan. In December 1961, however, the USAF decided to go straight from air-launched subsonic and supersonic flight tests to the first, unmanned orbital flights.

Dyna-Soar received a boost from the success of the X-15, which had romped ahead after overcoming its engine troubles. The XLR-99 had flown in November 1960, and within a year USAF pilot Bob White had taken the X-15 to 4,093mph, or Mach 6.04. The engineers knew that the mathematical predictions that they had used to design the X-20 were reasonably accurate in the hypersonic regime.

But Dyna-Soar was undermined by other developments. By 1962, the first reconnaissance satellites—the os-

Fastest of all 1960s air-breathers was the 15,000-mile-range D-21 drone, seen perched on the back of an A-12. Lockheed

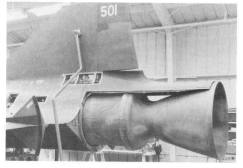

This rocket-like nozzle was fitted to the D-21's Marquardt RJ43 ramjet engine. With its extremely high fixed expansion ratio, it is tightly optimized for high speeds and high altitudes. via Jim Goodall

tensibly civilian *Discoverer* and the military satellite and missile observation system (SAMOS)—had been made to work.

Then, in 1963, the USAF and Soviet Union signed a treaty limiting the military uses of space. It outlawed offensively armed space vehicles, recognized that space surveillance was legal, and prohibited physical interference with satellites. Most of the Dyna-Soar's military missions had been eliminated.

The USAF was under budgetary and political pressure, and Dyna-Soar was an expensive project with suddenly marginal applications. NASA, on the way to the moon, was not interested in taking over the program, and it was canceled late in 1963.

The X-15 and Dyna-Soar projects had investigated solutions to some of the challenges of hypersonic flight, but these rocket-driven vehicles did not address one of the toughest problems: the need for more efficient power.

During the 1950s, turbojet engines moved quickly toward their speed limits. It was clear that, beyond Mach 3, the ramjet was the most logical next step. Pioneer Roy Marquardt, a Curtiss-Wright Corporation team, and others pitched ramjets for vehicles that would be faster than would be possible with contemporary turbojets. In fact, ramjets had been adopted for three vehicles in the Mach 3 class before 1950.

The most successful of all the US high-speed research aircraft was without a doubt the X-15. Sturdy and reliable, the X-15s flew more than 300 flights to top speeds of Mach 7.4 and a maximum altitude of 354,000 feet. Rockwell International

North American designed the X-15 with a deliberately conservative aerodynamic configuration, with a short tapered wing and separate swept tail. As the company's knowledge of delta wings increased, however, North American proposed modified, delta-winged X-15s with lower drag and higher stability. Rockwell

One was the Navaho, with two Curtiss-Wright ramjets; another was the Boeing XF-99 Bomarc, which despite its designation was not a fighter but a monster surface-to-air missile with Marquardt RJ43 ramjets. In both cases, the designers used large, separable rocket boosters to accelerate the vehicles to almost Mach 2 before lighting the ramjets; this meant that the ramjets never operated far outside their most efficient speed regime and gave the missiles a very respectable range.

The third ramjet project was the Republic XF-103, ordered into develop-

Advanced X-15 studies continued into the mid-1960s, culminating in this stretched aircraft (10 feet longer than the basic X-15) with a 75-degree delta wing and tip-mounted fins. A larger rocket engine—possibly Rocketdyne's LR-105—is installed.

ment in 1951. This was a manned interceptor, designed in anticipation that the Soviet Union would eventually build a large fleet of supersonic bombers. As a manned aircraft, it needed power over a larger flight envelope than the missiles, so it was designed with a unique powerplant that combined an afterburning turbojet (a Wright J67), developed from the British Bristol Aeroplane Company's Olympus and a Curtiss-Wright XRJ55 ramjet, using the same inlet and exhaust system. On pure ramjet power, the XF-103 was expected to attain no less than Mach 3.7, or 2,450mph.

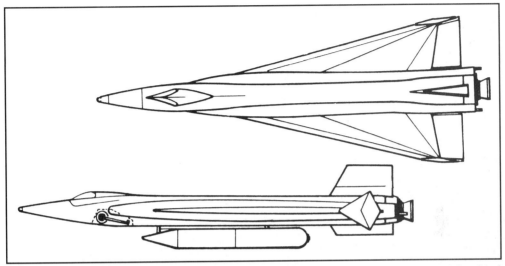

The delta X-15 would have had a center-line drop tank to increase motor burn time, speed, and altitude. Although it would be radically different in shape from the X-15,

North American planned to use the third X-15 airframe as a basis for the new aircraft. Rockwell

The XF-103's radical turbo-ramjet engine was ground-tested in 1956, but the project was canceled the following year in favor of the more conventional North American F-108 Rapier, a Mach 3 turbojet design. The Navaho was canceled around the same time, and Curtiss-Wright soon withdrew from the ramjet business.

Roy Marquardt's company kept its focus on what the company's leader thought would be the engine of the future. The Marquardt plant at Van Nuys, California, expanded to house a unique range of high-Mach test chambers. Marquardt's engines were classified by their diameter: the 28 inch RJ43 for the Bomarc was followed in tests by a 36 inch engine, and a 48 inch ramjet was also planned. Since thrust was proportional to the airflow, and hence to the square of the diameter, the 48 inch ramjet had three times the power of the 28 inch engine.

The Marquardt engines were test-flown between 1951 and 1959 on sixty-one Lockheed X-7 unmanned test vehicles. The highly successful X-7 program included one flight that reached a maximum Mach number of 4.31.

The McDonnell Aircraft Corporation, meanwhile, was working with the Applied Physics Laboratory (APL) of Johns Hopkins University on ramjet-powered surface-to-air missiles. APL was largely funded by the Navy, and had played a key role in developing the Terrier, Tartar, and Talos missiles. In the late 1950s, anticipating that Navy ships would be threatened by Soviet supersonic bombers armed with stand-off missiles. APL and Mc-Donnell Douglas developed a monster ramjet-powered SAM called Typhon. Some Typhon test vehicles reached Mach 5—the problem was that they went out so far and so fast that no radar could track and control them.

It was the Lockheed X-7, however, that led directly to the fastest and highest-flying aircraft ever used operationally. By 1990, that aircraft was still highly classified, almost twenty years after its last attempted operation.

On May 1, 1960, Francis G. Powers' U-2 spyplane was shot down over Sverdlovsk in the Soviet Union, ending almost four years of clandestine overflights in an international scandal. President Dwight Eisenhower, misled by his advisors, tried to maintain that the U-2 had drifted off course during an upper-atmosphere research

North American proposed to launch the modified X-15 from the back of the XB-70: as Lockheed found with the A-12/D-21 combination, the airflow above a delta wing is uniform and benign even at Mach 3 and conducive to a clean separation. (The notorious A-12/D-21 collision was due to different factors.) Launched at 70,000 feet and Mach 3, the X-15 would have attained Mach 8. Rockwell

In the era of Apollo, funds for high-speed research would support only a more modest enhancement of the X-15, with a small fuselage stretch, external fuel tanks, and an ablative coating to withstand higher *temperatures. Under the tail is a small experimental scramjet engine, fueled by liquid hydrogen carried in the ventral tail.* Rockwell

flight, but Powers' own confession and the espionage kit on his aircraft gave him away. Eisenhower felt that he had no choice but to ban manned reconnaissance flights over the Soviet Union.

The loophole in the ban—unmanned overflights were not mentioned—was designed to protect the new reconnaissance satellites. But the ban did remove the primary mission of the A-12 Oxcart, which Lockheed and the Central Intelligence Agency were developing to replace the U-2.

To comply with the ban on manned overflights, Lockheed proposed to add a second stage to the A-

12: an unmanned reconnaissance vehicle using some of the aerodynamic and materials technology developed for the A-12, but with an even higher speed and phenomenal range. Around 1962, Lockheed was authorized to proceed with this system under the codename Tagboard, with the company designation D-21.

The D-21 was to be launched from the back of the A-12. It was an expendable, single-mission vehicle, and it was completely automatic from the moment it was launched. Its blended-delta body could accommodate a camera and an ejectable film pod. The engine was a Marquardt RJ43-MA-11,

Encouraged by the success of the X-15, the USAF and Boeing designed the X-20 Dyna-Soar, a small, single-pilot recoverable spaceplane that could land on a conventional runway. Note that the sharp *leading edges of the X-15 have given way to a bluff-edged delta, better able to resist the high temperatures and pressures caused by hypersonic flow stagnation.* Boeing

This photo shows Dyna-Soar without the jettisonable shield that protected the windshield during launch and re-entry. Boeing

actually removed from a surplus Bomarc missile; the fuel was the same JP-7 that was used on the A-12 itself.

In operational use, the A-12 would launch the D-21 at almost Mach 3, around 80,000 feet. The D-21 would accelerate and climb to near Mach 4 and 100,000 feet as fuel burned off, using its inertial navigation system to follow a pre-programmed track to the target, where the camera would operate automatically.

The D-21 would exit hostile airspace, fly to a predetermined point over international waters, and glide to a lower speed and altitude where the film pod could be safely ejected. An explosive charges would blow the top-secret aircraft into tiny, unrecognizable fragments. All that would be left would be the film pod, descending by parachute and transmitting its location with a beacon. A homing device would guide a C-119 or C-130 transport to the retrieval zone, where it would snag the parachute lines with a trapeze and haul the film pod on board.

The most extraordinary feature of the D-21, however, was its range. This figure was officially classified until very recently. It was a shock to observers when, at a 1987 meeting, Skunk Works chief Ben Rich disclosed that the D-21 had an endurance of no less than four hours at Mach 3.8 (2,520mph), translating into a total range of 10,000 miles—equal to that of a B-52. That this was possible, even with a small, fast vehicle, was an illuminating lesson in the value of high speed: the D-21 showed, for those who were cleared to know about it, that speed does not necessarily mean inefficiency.

The D-21 was an elaborate system that did not quite work. Air-launching an eight-ton vehicle at Mach 3 could never be regarded as free from risk. In May 1966, on the sixth launch attempt, a D-21 suffered a control failure and collided with the A-12 mother ship. Both A-12 crew members ejected, but the observer was drowned.

The supersonic air launch was decreed unacceptable for operational use, and the D-21 program stopped while a new, rocket-boosted version was developed, to be launched from a B-52H. In the early 1970s, two B-52Hs were modified to launch the D-21B and were based alongside the SR-71 Blackbirds at Beale Air Force Base, California.

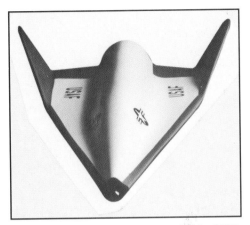

Although Dyna-Soar was canceled in 1963, similar technology was applied to unmanned hypersonic glide vehicles (HGVs) launched by Atlas or Titan boosters for nuclear strike and other missions. First tested in the early 1960s, HGVs received renewed attention in the 1980s as a means of evading defenses and attacking mobile targets. Loral

Several operational reconnaissance flights were attempted over China and the Soviet Union, but none was successful: the D-21s disappeared, or missed their targets, or the film-recovery system failed. After President Richard Nixon agreed to cease overflights of China in 1972, the program was terminated.

The D-21 achieved its extraordinary performance using relatively conventional fuel and surplus engines. Researchers knew that much more was achievable. In the early 1960s, the strands of ramjet, boost-glide, and rocket research were briefly pulled together in a visionary study for a so-called Aerospaceplane: a vehicle that could take off and land from a normal runway and either ascend into orbit or cruise in the high hypersonic regime. It would therefore combine the near-unlimited endurance of the satellite with the aircraft's ability to maneuver and change course. It used radical new engines—neither ramjets nor rockets but an amalgam of both—and would have been fueled with liquid hydrogen, something that Lockheed's CL-400 had proven possible.

The challenges that the Aerospaceplane posed inspired a great deal of research and study, which in turn advanced the art of hypersonic design. But it relied on engine concepts that had not even been proved in a labora-tory, and it probably could not have been built with the materials of the day.

Above all, there was no money to even start the project. Planners who had dreamed of fleets of Mach 3 fighters and bombers never saw their visions realized. The only Mach 3 aircraft to enter service were the Lockheed Blackbirds and the MiG-25 interceptors that were built to catch them. The USAF never even fielded a truly supersonic strategic bomber after the B-58; the B-1 was designed for Mach

Lockheed's classified air-launched HGV project from the mid-1980s resembled this *artist's impression produced by General Dynamics. GD*

2, but is only marginally supersonic in its service form.

Mach 2.5 turned out to be a plateau for fighter speeds, and the most successful fighter of the 1970s and 1980s, the F-16, could barely touch Mach 2. Even the new F-22 probably has a lower maximum Mach number than the aging F-4.

There were all sorts of reasons for this reversal. One was money. The aircraft of each generation were not only much faster than their predecessors, they were also bigger and more expensive. The F-4 fighter of the late 1950s was as heavy as a B-17 Fortress, and the YF-12 was more than twice the size of an F-4. The cost went up even faster.

Another reason, though, was that many people—including President John Kennedy's secretary of defense, Robert McNamara, and his team of analysts—believed that faster, higher-

In the late 1960s, Lockheed and the USAF Flight Dynamics Laboratory built a full-scale mockup of a hypersonic research aircraft using the FDL-5 shape, bearing an uncanny resemblance to the vehicle seen over the North Sea in August 1989. This configuration used a stabilization technique called "compression sharing" to dispense with the large wing-tip fins of the X-20 and other aircraft. It also featured flip-out wings to reduce its landing speed and retractable fairings in front of the split windshield. USAF via David Selegan

The FDL-5 was designed to be air-launched from a B-52. Fuel for initial acceleration was to be carried in two conformal tanks forming a V-shaped collar around the vehicle. USAF via David Selegan

flying aircraft simply would be outpaced by faster, better surface-to-air missiles. At least, that was what their computer analyses seemed to show. Experience proved them wrong, however; missile systems have, in many ways, yet to fulfil the confident predictions of the late 1950s and early 1960s. But their decisions were law at the time.

Then, aeronautical research took a blow from another quarter. In April

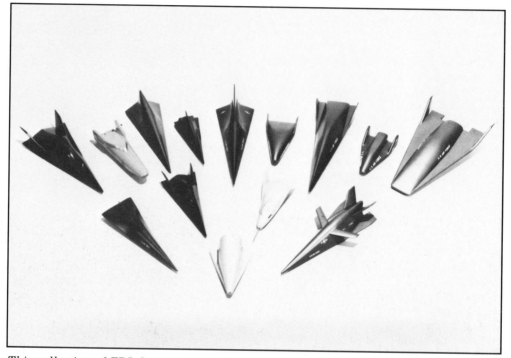

This collection of FDL hypersonic study shapes includes the FDL-5 (front row left), the FDL-8, used for the X-24B (back row left), and a couple of boost-glide vehicles (center front and back row, second from right). The spatula-nosed shape (back row right) is an Aerospaceplane concept; as in the case of the latest X-30 configuration, the wide nose provides better compression for the under-fuselage ramjet engines. Eight out of the fourteen shapes correspond exactly to the North Sea sighting of August 1989. USAF via David Selegan

1961, a Soviet rocket shot Yuri Gagarin's Vostok capsule into orbit. Within months, a monster was conceived that, once grown to full size, ate almost the entire budget of the X-15's sponsor—the National Advisory Committee for Aeronautics, renamed the National Aeronautics and Space Administration. NASA went to the moon, and high-speed flight research was left with the table scraps.

Between them, the change in military priorities and the expansion of space research eliminated any chance of building another new aircraft for high-speed flight research. Without flight-test vehicles, the high-speed regime was unexplored territory, a land where only models, studies, and theoretical research could go.

Fortunately, some of the programs that escaped the axe generated very useful new data. In particular, the USAF Flight Dynamics Laboratory (FDL) devised new and more efficient shapes for hypersonic vehicles. It had been known that conventional shapes, with a separate or slightly blended wing and body, were adequate aerodynamically but did not work well from a thermal standpoint; they suffered from high localized heating loads, and the wings were too hot to hold fuel.

In the late 1950s, NASA aerodynamicists devised radical shapes with no wings at all. These "lifting bodies" were short and rounded, and used combinations of flat and curved surfaces to generate lift and control the distribution of aerodynamic heat. It appeared that they would perform effectively at very high speeds; the question was whether they would behave well enough at low speeds to be able to land on a runway.

In 1963, Northrop Corporation delivered a 1,200 pound piloted wooden lifting body, the M2-F1, to NASA. It was a glider, but it was followed by the rocket-powered, all-metal M2-F2 and the HL-10, with similar systems but a different aerodynamic shape: the M2-F1 and M2-F2 were flat on top, while the HL-10 was flat underneath.

NASA researchers, with an institutional bias towards "blunt body" shapes for re-entry vehicles, promoted round-fronted lifting-body shapes like the Martin-Marietta

X-24A. The low-speed handling qualities of these shapes varied from interesting to hazardous. USAF

The X-24C studies embraced a range of solutions, including this air-launched, unmanned vehicle carried by NASA's YF-12C. (At that time, NASA was very keen on using sub-scale, unmanned research aircraft.) None of them was funded, at least in the white world. Lockheed

A wind-tunnel model of the X-24C, proposed by the FDL and NASA in 1975. (Physically, this aircraft would have had nothing in common with the X-24A and X-24B.) Note, again, the 75-degree delta shape. USAF via David Selegan

The results of these tests were mixed. The M2-F2 may be best known for its role in the television series *The Six Million Dollar Man*, which featured the prototype's May 1967 crash in its opening credits. The aircraft crashed due to roll oscillations. By the time NASA's now-dominant astronaut lobby chose its next megaproject—a reusable space vehicle—the necessary aerodynamic technology to make it work well did not exist. The shuttle ended up with a rather basic aerodynamic shape that combined low risk with uninspiring performance.

The NASA-designed lifting-body shapes were short and blunt because they were designed as controlled, runway-recovered re-entry vehicles. Ultimate aerodynamic efficiency was not particularly important since they were not designed to make long atmospheric glides or maneuvers, except to position themselves for landing, and transonic drag was not important because the vehicle would be lofted through the transonic zone in a zero-lift state, on a rocket. On the other hand, weight was important because it determined how much payload could be launched with a given booster.

The Air Force, in a series of tests under the ASSET and PRIME programs, demonstrated small unmanned lifting-body re-entry vehicles with blunt-body shapes. However, the service also supported a mid-1960s McDonnell Aircraft program to demonstrate a hypersonic vehicle capable of long-range, high-speed flight through the atmosphere. This was the Boost Glide Research Vehicle (BGRV).

The BGRV was a slender-delta-shaped vehicle launched by an Atlas booster. Because it flew in the atmosphere, it could be maneuvered throughout its flight and could be programed to hit a target from any direction; because it flew much lower than a satellite or a ballistic ICBM warhead, it would be much closer to impact when it was detected. One one test, a BGRV was released from an Atlas over the northwestern United States and was deliberately splashed into the ocean off Japan. "If we hadn't done that it would have carried on past Australia," an engineer recalls.

The Flight Dynamics Laboratory's later shapes—FDL-5, FDL-6, FDL-7, and FDL-8—were designed with sustained hypersonic flight, both gliding and powered, in mind as well as re-entry. Even at high hypersonic speeds, they were capable of lift-to-drag ratios as high as 3:1. They differed in their fin and tail arrangements, but in plan view, they were all quite similar: They were plain seventy-five-degree triangles.

In late 1968, the USAF decided to modify a surplus blunt-body vehicle, a Martin SV-5J, into a rocket-powered aircraft with the FDL-8 shape. Extra panels and fins were built on to the aircraft, which was redesignated the X-24B and made its first flight in August 1973. In a thirty-six-flight program ending in November 1975, the X-24B attained a maximum speed of Mach 1.76, but, more importantly, demonstrated a high degree of controllability despite its radical shape and dramatic leading-edge sweep angle. It was the only lifting-body aircraft to land on a conventional runway, rather than the Edwards lake bed.

Further hypersonic research, however, required a new vehicle. Plans for such an aircraft took shape as the X-24B flight-test program drew to a close; although it was a new aircraft, NASA and the USAF assigned it the designation X-24C. The X-24C used a modified FDL-8 shape. Powered by either a Thiokol XLR-99 or a Rocketdyne LR-105, it was to be about as fast as the X-15, with a top speed of Mach 7.4 (6,630mph), and would have been about equal in weight (56,000 pounds) to the stretched, drop-tank-equipped X-15A-2. Like the X-15 and X-24B, it was to be air-launched from NASA's NB-52B.

The X-24C was not designed primarily to extend the frontiers of absolute or sustained speed. Rather, it was designed as a flying testbed for

The FDL also investigated a Maneuvering Re-entry Research Vehicle (MRRV) to explore flight regimes from Mach 8 to orbit. This version, with folding outer wings and tail, would have been launched into orbit by the Shuttle. Smaller versions could have been launched by a Titan expendable booster. USAF via David Selegan

ramjet or scramjet engines, which were to be mounted under the rear of the body. The goal was to test the scramjets during about forty seconds of high-speed level flight.

In 1975, NASA planned to continue X-24C studies until 1978, select a scramjet and aircraft design in that year, and fly the first of two X-24Cs in 1981. The two aircraft would carry out a 100 sortie flight-test program over ten years, finishing in 1991.

Some companies proposed alternative approaches to the X-24C requirement. Lockheed's X-24C-L301 study envisaged a much smaller vehicle, carried on the back of one of NASA's YF-12 Blackbirds and launched like the D-21. The Lockheed vehicle would have been much smaller than the B-52 launched X-24C; however, the YF-12 could have carried a 25,000 pound payload to Mach 3.2, and the much higher launch speed and altitude would compensate for the vehicle's smaller size.

But it was not to happen—at least apparently. The X-24C was referred to, for a while, as the National Hypersonic Flight Research Facility (NHFRF), but NASA and the USAF never found money to build prototypes.

Boeing's Air Launched Sortie Vehicle (ALSV) design study was a recoverable orbiting vehicle carried on a modified 747.

The Space Shuttle engine in the 747's tail allowed it to release the orbiter in a 60-degree climb.

This Rockwell artist's concept from 1980 is typical of ideas for a transatmospheric vehicle (TAV), with a normal operating regime extending from the outer edges of the atmosphere into space. A variety of unconventional engines were considered for TAVs, including hybrid turbo-rockets. Rockwell

Historian Rene Francillon, however, in a definitive survey of Lockheed aircraft published in 1982, reported that Lockheed had already flown an experimental aircraft capable of sustained flight at Mach 6. This could have been a black-world extrapolation of the air-launched X-24C-L301 project.

The next public references to hypersonic aircraft appeared in 1982, when Boeing released details of an Air Launched Sortie Vehicle (ALSV) which it was studying under a US Air Force contract. The ALSV orbiter was an FDL-8 shaped boost-glide vehicle, about the size of an F-16 or Dyna-Soar, weighing 22,000 pounds without fuel. Like Dyna-Soar, it could be flown with or without a pilot, and it was intended to support a variety of military missions, although reconnaissance was the most obvious example.

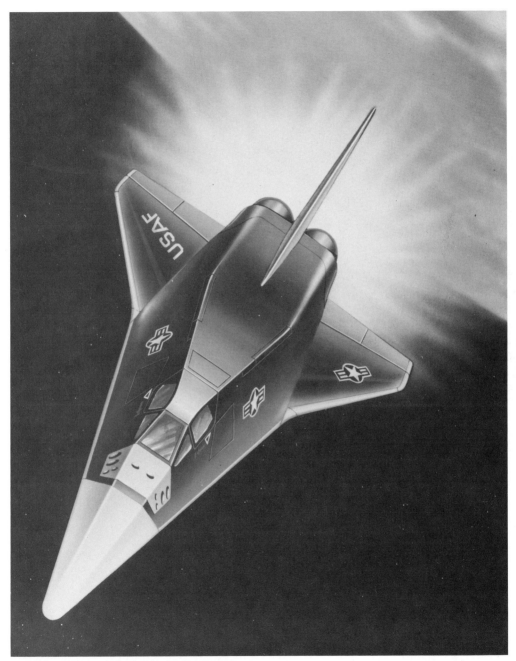

A later version of the Rockwell TAV study, with a single seat and a different propulsion system. Rockwell

Also from the Rockwell project office was this Shuttle-like vehicle launched from a 747. Unlike the Boeing study, the 747 does not have a booster engine and it is equipped with a V-tail to clear the wake of the orbiter. No inlet is visible, but a hybrid air-breathing/rocket-cycle engine would probably be essential for this kind of vehicle. Rockwell

The ALSV was not designed to carry a large payload. Its advantages were that it would be mobile, flexible, independent of rocket-launch sites, and almost entirely reusable. To achieve these goals, the designers created a system in which the orbiter perched on the back of a highly modified Boeing 747. The 747's fuselage would hold 100 tons of liquid hydrogen (LH_2) and liquid oxygen (LOX) in well-insulated tanks, and a single Rocketdyne space shuttle main engine would be installed in the tail. The orbiter itself would be fitted with seven uprated Pratt & Whitney RL-10 engines—versions of a reliable, proven LH_2-LOX rocket—and would carry a large external fuel tank.

To launch the ALSV, the 747 would climb to 22,000 feet and fill the vehicle's light, uninsulated external fuel tank in the cold upper air. Then, the mother ship would fire its rocket engine and climb at a sixty-degree angle to 37,000 feet before releasing the orbiter, which would continue into orbit. The launch point could be any-where in the world because the 747 could be refueled in flight to give it ef-fectively unlimited range. ALSV, Boe-ing, and the USAF said, could be oper-ational as early as 1988, but it was not funded.

Instead, the USAF continued with a series of studies under the Advanced Military Spaceflight Capability (AMSC) program. By 1984, this work

Launching a hypersonic aircraft from a conventional runway can be a problem, be-cause short wings and high fuel loads can mean high takeoff speeds. This Rockwell concept uses what might almost be called a

"flying sled": Exhaust from five jet engines is trapped underneath the wings and lifts the entire vehicle on a cushion of air before it accelerates to flying speed. Rockwell

This 1985 USAF study for a single-stage-to-orbit TAV features six combined-cycle engines on the sides of a conical body. Optimized for reconnaissance or strike, with a small, low-volume payload, the design emphasized light weight. USAF

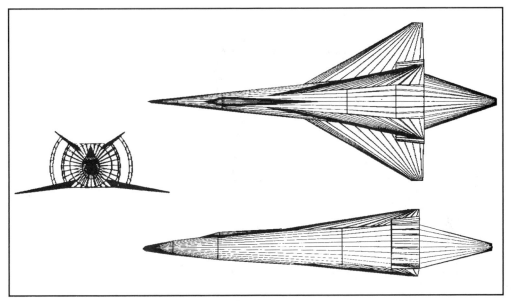

The USAF TAV study featured a conical aft body that acted as an expansion ramp for the side-mounted engines. USAF

an operational TAV before the late 1990s. Hypersonic hardware still appeared to be on the back burner.

Or was it? The MRRV, the FDL-5 shape, and other hypersonic aircraft discussed in the 1983 paper shared one distinguishing feature: a plain, triangular planform with a leading-edge sweep of seventy-five degrees, just like the aircraft that Chris Gibson saw over the North Sea in August 1989.

Chapter 3

The Hypersonic Revolution

The plans, comprising some thirty separate patents, each essential to the working of the whole...

—Conan Doyle, *The Bruce-Partington Plans*

There are three reasons why the North Sea sketch is the most persuasive rendition of Aurora to appear so far. The first is the observer's qualifications. The second is the fact that the North Sea aircraft corresponds almost exactly in shape and size to hypersonic reconnaissance aircraft studied in the 1970s and 1980s by McDonnell Douglas and the Air Force. Third, the North Sea aircraft looks totally unlike anything else. No aircraft other than a highly supersonic vehicle, or a test aircraft for such a vehicle, has ever been built or studied with such a planform.

The hypersonic regime has some unique characteristics. On a graph of speed and altitude, the practical flight envelope looks like a narrow, curving funnel: At any given Mach number, the permissible altitude range is small. On the low and fast side of the envelope, friction generates too much heat for the vehicle to endure for more than seconds; this part of the envelope belongs to short-time-of-flight "hypervelocity" missiles.

On the high and slow side, there is not enough dynamic air pressure (the

pressure rise caused by the vehicle's speed) to sustain level flight or to feed air-breathing engines. The shuttle operates in this regime in its vertical, rocket-boosted ascent.

At hypersonic speeds, aerodynamic design gives way to aero-thermodynamic design. Not only must the vehicle generate minimum drag, but it also must be free of design features that give rise to concentrations of heat; the design must spread the heat over the structure, preferably in places where there is enough mass to dissipate it quickly. Conventional, thin-section wings and tail surfaces must be eliminated or made as small as possible.

Thermal management is critical. Skin friction pumps heat energy into the aircraft, and it must be pumped out again if the vehicle is to have any endurance. The only way to do this is to heat the fuel before it is fed to the engine, and dump the heat overboard through the exhaust. This, of course, is done on Mach 2–3 supersonic cruisers such as the Concorde and SR-71, but it is more severe on a hypersonic vehicle.

The cooling capacity of the fuel must be used carefully and efficiently, or the vehicle's range and endurance will be limited by heating rather than fuel capacity.

Cooling is only a part of thermal management. Acceleration, attitude changes, and maneuvers all change the heat loading and the heat distribution; accurate flight control is essential. Also, even the best cooling scheme does not eliminate the need for high-temperature materials.

The conventional turbojet engine is out of the picture. Any jet inlet system is designed to decelerate the incoming airstream to a speed that the engine can handle; in the case of a jet, this speed may be barely transonic. At the same time, the air is compressed and heated. Above Mach 4–5, this process generates such high temperatures at the inlet face that no turbine engine could compress it further and survive. Palliatives such as bleeding much of the airflow past the engine, which works on the SR-71, will not work at such speeds.

The basic principle of any hypersonic propulsion system dates back to France in the 1930s, when Rene Leduc patented the aero-thermodynamic duct, or ramjet. Like any air-breathing internal combustion engine, the ramjet operates on a compression-combustion-expansion cycle, and produces net power because the expansion releases more energy than is required by the compression process.

The basic aerodynamic challenge in a ramjet-powered hypersonic design—and no engine other than the ramjet has been shown to work efficiently at such speeds—is that the ramjet engines provide enormous thrust, but that they also generate enormous drag in the process of slowing down and compressing the Mach 6 airstream. Net thrust, or the difference between thrust and drag, is only a small portion of the total thrust, so a small increase in drag can wipe it out completely. When the net thrust reaches zero, the aircraft has reached its maximum speed.

The way to make the ramjet engine efficient is to spread it over the entire length of the vehicle. The SR-71 did this to some extent because its engines breathed air that had already been compressed by the shock wave off the nose. In a hypersonic ramjet aircraft, the entire underside of the forward body is a ramp that compresses the air, and the entire underside of the tail is an exhaust nozzle. The ramjet "cowl" beneath the body is just the high-pressure section of the engine.

So much compressed air underneath the body serves another purpose: it holds the airplane up. For a hypersonic aircraft, wings are superfluous and, at Mach 6, a positive embarrassment, causing excess drag and requiring extra cooling.

The ramjets need a large inlet area to provide the high thrust needed for Mach 6 cruise. As a result, the engines occupy a large area beneath the vehicle. At the same time, the need to accommodate a large-volume fuel drives the aircraft toward an all-body shape.

High speeds have tended to be associated with short range, but—as was seen with the small, 15,000 mile range D-21 drone—this is not necessarily true. One reason for the D-21's great range is that it was a "point design," with a very narrow flight envelope. It did not need to fly below Mach 3, so its simple, fixed inlet and exhaust were designed to operate efficiently in its design flight regime. The inlet cone, for example, was gradually flared so that the air moving over it generated a series of relatively weak shocks at the D-21's cruising speed. The D-21 did not need fuel to climb to its cruising height, it had no landing gear or recovery gear, and it needed to be strong enough for only one flight, so its structure was very light.

A B-52, with its long-span wing, has an inherently high lift-to-drag ratio (about 19:1) at its normal subsonic cruising speed. A delta like the D-21, with the skin friction and wave drag associated with its supersonic cruising speed, will be hard put to achieve a lift-to-drag ratio of 6:1. The B-52 seems to be more efficient—but the missing factor is speed.

A faster aircraft uses energy (drag) to resist gravity (lift) at a higher rate than a slower aircraft, but it covers the ground faster, so it uses energy for a shorter period. The classic Breguet range equation allows for this: the lift-to-drag ratio is multiplied by the Mach number (M x L/D). The M(L/D) for the Mach 0.85 B-52 is 16:1; for the D-21, it is 23:1.

Engine efficiency is also a factor. Overall pressure ratio (OPR) is a benchmark of efficiency for a turbojet or ramjet engine, just as compression ratio is an indicator of efficiency for a piston engine. Even today, an OPR of 35:1 is a mark of a high-efficiency subsonic turbine engine. But at Mach 3.8, a simple ramjet like the RJ43 could generate an OPR of more than 40:1 (an unattainable figure for a turbine engine in the 1960s) with no moving parts.

Of course, an efficient high-speed shape would be of little use if the aircraft could not take off and land at normal speeds. At such low speeds, Aurora draws on the results of the lift-ing-body research done by NASA and the USAF in the 1960s and 1970s. There are two main factors that make these wingless shapes practical at normal takeoff and landing speeds. First, the entire body is a lifting surface, and it has a great deal of area. Second, like the Concorde's wing, the sharply swept leading edge generates a powerful vortex at high angles of attack, which clings to the leading edge and boosts the wing's lift.

Stability and control are challenges for a hypersonic aircraft. The forces acting on the forward part of the body—the inlets and body sides—are extremely large. Ramjet unstarts, where a shock wave that is normally contained within the duct pops out of it, can cause rapid increases in drag that are not necessarily symmetrical. But the all-body shape does not provide an ideal environment for conventional control surfaces. There is not much span available for elevons, which are also on the back of a long-chord wing. Vortices from the forebody can blanket, buffet, or otherwise interfere with the verticals at high angles of attack.

This is why the outer wings of some hypersonic designs, including the National Aerospace Plane (NASP) design, have become all-moving surfaces for pitch and roll control. The size of the verticals is a matter for debate. McDonnell Douglas' studies have rather large vertical surfaces, above and below the body, which help with stability by acting as endplates for the all-moving wing tips; NASP, and a NASA study disclosed in early 1993, have quite small surfaces. The FDL-5 shape, which formed the basis for a USAF-Lockheed study, was carefully contoured according to a principle dubbed "compression sharing," and used only a single vertical fin.

Control problems may also be eased by using unconventional devices to handle the most difficult cases. In some McDonnell Douglas designs, small retractable "mustache" wing tips were used to help rotate the aircraft for takeoff, allowing the elevons to be made smaller. Also, a highly swept all-

Described as a NASP design when it was released in 1986, this McDonnell Douglas concept is actually representative of the company's Mach 6 hypersonic studies. McDonnell Douglas

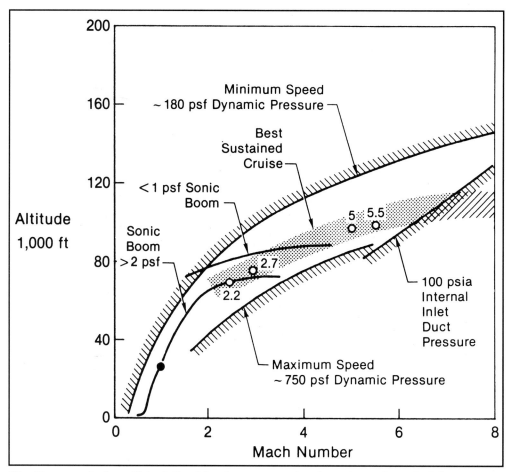

The "hypersonic funnel" is defined by the facts that the atmosphere is less dense as altitude increases, and that the movement of the vehicle causes dynamic pressure as it forces air out of its path. Above the top "minimum speed" line, there is too little air pressure to lift the vehicle or make air-breathing engines work; below the bottom line, pressures are too high for the structure. There is a high-speed limit on conventional ramjets, where the inlet pressure exceeds 100 pounds per square inch and weight becomes a problem. Sonic boom overpressures drop by more than half when the cruise altitude increases from 60,000 feet (Concorde) to 80,000 feet (SR-71). A hypersonic vehicle at 100,000 feet may not leave any perceptible boom on the ground. McDonnell Douglas

body could be a suitable application for active vortex control. By using either a very small movable surface or an air jet to modify the leading-edge vortex, researchers have shown that it is possible to generate very powerful yaw and roll forces. Doing so predictably and controllably is a challenge.

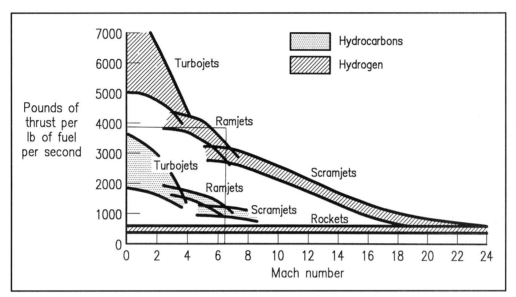

Pounds of thrust per lb of fuel per second (y-axis)
Mach number (x-axis)

Legend: Hydrocarbons / Hydrogen

Most engine people talk in terms of specific fuel consumption; hypersonic and rocket designers talk about specific impulse—pounds of thrust per pound of fuel per second. Turbojets are very efficient, but do not work much above Mach 3 because the temperatures are too high for the turbine.

Ramjets rule from Mach 4 to Mach 7, but they produce no thrust at standstill and little below Mach 2. Hydrogen provides high specific impulse, because of its immense energy content per unit of weight. Pratt & Whitney

Aurora appears small when seen from directly below. It may be as much as twenty feet shorter than an SR-71. Size, however, is very deceptive.

Structurally, the all-body shape is highly efficient, mainly because there are no aerodynamic freeloaders like a conventional fuselage, and the average cross-sectional area is large. It offers a great deal of volume—space for useful load, equipment, and fuel—inside a structure that is light, efficient, and compact and has a relatively small surface area to generate friction drag.

Aurora could weigh as much as 170,000 pounds fully loaded, but a clear two-thirds of its mass would be fuel, and it could be more. This compares with the 57 percent fuel fraction of the SR-71, which is good by most standards, even today's.

The choice of fuel is a basic consideration. As already noted, the fuel is used to cool the vehicle. At hypersonic speeds, however, even an exotic kerosene such as the JP-7 used by the SR-71 cannot absorb enough heat to meet the cooling requirements without breaking down chemically and clogging the fuel system.

There are a number of unusual hydrocarbon fuels that can absorb greater heat. Methylcyclohexane (MCH), for example, absorbs heat through a chemical reaction and breaks down into hydrogen and toluene, which can then be burned as fuel. For Aurora, though, the most

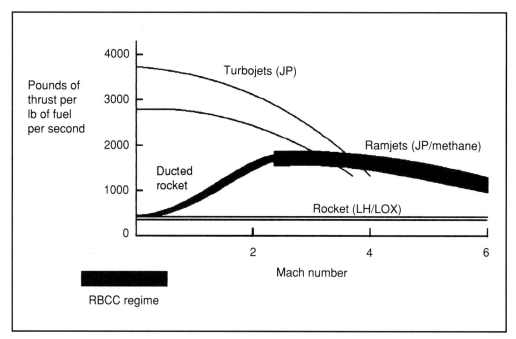

Pounds of thrust per lb of fuel per second

4000

3000

2000

1000

0

Turbojets (JP)

Ramjets (JP/methane)

Ducted rocket

Rocket (LH/LOX)

2   4   6

Mach number

RBCC regime

An expanded view of the lower left corner of the previous graph, this shows how an air-augmented or ducted rocket delivers higher specific impulse than a pure rocket *and can serve as the accelerator for a ram-jet. A turbojet is more efficient but much heavier.*

likely solution is a cryogenic fuel—a cold, liquefied gas. The Skunk Works knew a great deal about cryogenic fuels thanks to the CL-400 program, and had blown the dust off its records during the 1970s when it proposed to build an experimental hydrogen-fueled freighter based on the Lockheed Tri-Star jetliner. In 1981, cryogenics were more of a known quantity than exotic hydrocarbons.

The best candidate fuels identified so far are methane and hydrogen. Methane is abundant: it forms 85–95 percent of natural gas. It provides 15 percent more energy per pound than conventional hydrocarbon fuels, and can absorb more than four times as much heat. It is liquid at minus forty-three degrees Fahrenheit at atmospheric pressure.

Liquid hydrogen (LH_2), which is used on the shuttle, provides more energy and absorbs more heat per pound than any other fuel. It has more than twice the energy per pound of methane, and absorbs almost six times as much heat.

The snag with LH_2 is its very low density, one-third that of liquid methane. This means bigger fuel tanks, a larger, heavier airframe, and more drag. While LH_2 is the fuel of choice for a space vehicle (which accelerates quickly out of the atmosphere), studies have shown that methane is better for an aircraft cruising at Mach 5–7. For the same range and payload, the methane-fueled aircraft is smaller and lighter than an LH_2 aircraft. LH_2, with a boiling point of minus 420 degrees Fahrenheit, is also more difficult to store than methane.

Methane is easy to use as a fuel; in many places, cars and other vehicles have been adapted to burn liquid natural gas. On the ground, it can be stored in pressurized cylinders at ambient temperatures. McDonnell Douglas has studied in-flight refueling with liquid methane, and it poses no fundamental problems; a KC-135, modified with lightweight, insulated tanks on its main deck, could easily carry enough methane to fuel an eighty-ton aircraft.

Because the liquid fuel wants to be a gas, the Aurora designers have some novel options in engine design. As noted, there is little disagreement that the ramjet is the most efficient means of propulsion in the cruise. It is also simple, in principle: air is forced into the inlet by the movement of the vehicle, compressed, and mixed with fuel. The mixture is ignited and allowed to expand, producing thrust.

The ramjet is fundamentally different from other engines in that the air is compressed only by the forward movement of the entire engine, rather than by pistons or rotating airfoils. Any moving parts in the gas stream are there to modulate the flow, not to add energy to it (like a jet's compressor) or to take it away (like a turbine).

Consequently, the ramjet has two basic and unique attributes. The first is that zero airspeed equals zero power. Any ramjet-powered vehicle needs an accelerator—another thrust source that can push it to a speed where the ramjet will operate.

The second is that the ramjet's power and efficiency are proportional to speed. Like a piston engine or a turbine, the ramjet's statistics—power-to-weight ratio, power-to-frontal-area ratio, and fuel efficiency—all improve as the overall pressure ratio improves because it can do more work by pumping the same amount of air.

The only way to improve pressure ratio in a ramjet is to increase its speed. It follows, therefore, that any ramjet-powered vehicle has a critical speed and altitude at which the ramjet alone will provide enough power to overcome the vehicle's drag.

Without complicated moving parts, though, a ramjet cannot operate efficiently over a wide speed range. Pressure and volume are inversely related (Boyle's law). If a ramjet is to operate efficiently, the areas of its inlet, duct, and nozzle must vary according to the varying pressure of the gas stream as it moves through the engine. These areas can be varied, up to a point, but only by ramp and nozzle systems which become bigger and more complicated as the desired speed range increases.

Most hypersonic studies show that the vehicle needs an accelerator that can take it to a speed between Mach 2 and Mach 3. The Lockheed D-21 had a remarkably efficient engine, but it operated only in a narrow speed range, from Mach 2.8 to Mach 3.8, and needed a carrier aircraft or booster to reach that speed. Other high-speed ramjet vehicles—such as missiles or Bomarc—were designed to be boosted to Mach 2 or above before the booster dropped away.

The critical design case for the accelerator may be the transonic zone, around Mach 1. The vehicle is full of fuel, the ramjet cycle is barely operational, and drag hits a hump. Even the sleek SR-71 normally dives through

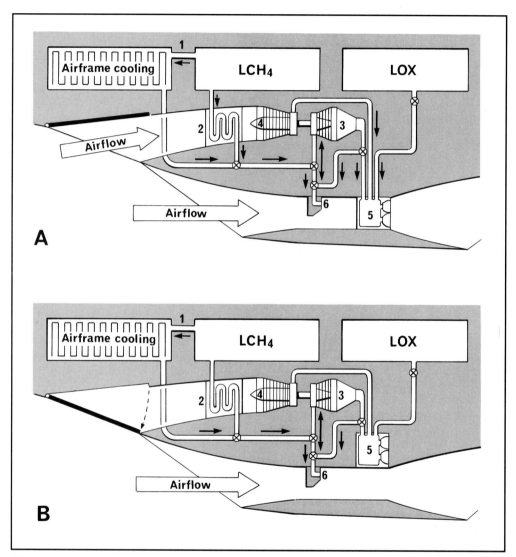

Upper: in a rocket-based combined-cycle engine, the liquid methane fuel flows through an airframe cooling circuit (1) or a heat exchanger (2) in the compressor air inlet. The expanding methane drives a turbine (3), which spins the compressor (4). The methane and compressed air are burned in rocket-type nozzles (5) inside the ramjet duct. At speeds below Mach 2.5, extra methane and LOX are supplied to the nozzles to generate more thrust. As the vehicle accelerates, more methane is supplied through the injector strut (6) and is burned in the airflow entering the ramjet. Lower: at cruising speeds, the compressor inlet and inlet heat exchanger are shut down, the compressor is uncoupled from the turbine, and the rocket nozzles are retracted. The hot fuel flows through the turbine to power the aircraft's systems and is fed to the ramjet through the injector strut (6).

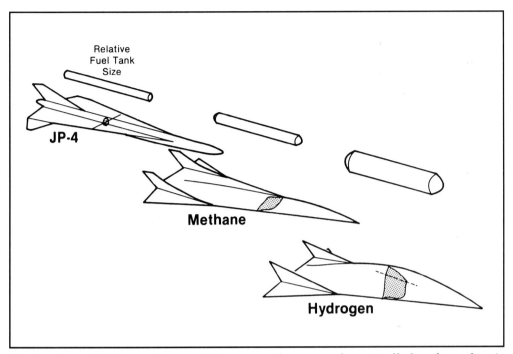

Relative Fuel Tank Size

JP-4

Methane

Hydrogen

Moving from JP-4 to methane and from methane to hydrogen increases the energy available from each pound of fuel, but means that less energy is available per unit of volume because methane and hy- *drogen are dramatically less dense than is JP-4. As shown here, the fuel tank gets larger; the entire airframe is bigger; and it needs more thrust, particularly for transonic acceleration.* McDonnell Douglas

the transonic regime, so as to break through it faster and save fuel.

The classic accelerator solution is the turbo-ramjet, in which a ramjet and a turbojet share a single inlet and nozzle, and the ramjet combustor is also the augmentor. The SR-71's J58 engine is close to a turbo-ramjet because much of the airflow in the cruise bypasses the bare engine; in a true turbo-ramjet, the process is carried further and the turbojet section is shut off completely at cruising speeds. The trouble with this solution, however, is that the turbojet and the variable inlet and nozzle are dead weight and volume in cruising flight, and the turbo-

jets are not small: they have to be powerful enough for takeoff, climb, and transonic acceleration. An Aurora-size vehicle would need at least four large fighter engines.

Hypersonic propulsion designers rate different engines according to a number called "specific impulse" (ISp). ISp is the amount of thrust, in pounds, produced by a pound of fuel in a second. Mathematically, the two pound quantities cancel each other out, so ISp is measured in seconds. ISp is really the same as specific fuel consumption (sfc), but it indicates the engine's thrust-producing potential more directly than an sfc number.

In 1978, Lockheed proposed to build a small number of modified L-1011 airliners as hydrogen-powered freighters, to evaluate the potential of liquid hydrogen as a future fuel for civil aviation. The hydrogen would have been carried in special extra fuselage sections fore and aft of the wing. The project showed that Lockheed considered cryogenic fuel to be suitable for regular aircraft operations. Lockheed

Any engine's specific impulse varies with speed. A 747's engine, for example, has an ISp of more than 5,000 seconds at Mach 0.9, but no ISp at all at higher speeds. A turbojet has high ISp at Mach 1, but it declines at Mach 2 and runs out above Mach 3. Rockets have very low ISp—400 seconds is considered good, even with liquid hydrogen—but it is constant from zero to Mach 25. Ramjet ISp starts at zero and gradually builds toward Mach 6. The trick is to find a combination of propulsion systems that provide a good ISp across the whole flight envelope, within acceptable weight limits.

There are two clues to the way in which the Aurora designers solved the problem. The National Aerospace Plane (NASP) team, open about most aspects of the program, has been tight-lipped about even the most basic principles of the "low-speed" or "accelerator" portion of the NASP engine. Officials have indicated that, in parts of the cycle, it works as a ducted rocket.

A ducted or air-augmented rocket is a way of boosting the rocket's ISp. The rocket exhaust is directed into an aerodynamic duct, draws air through the duct, and accelerates it. At low speeds, the larger mass flow and lower total exhaust velocity make the engine more efficient. Also, the rocket exhaust can be made fuel-rich by reducing the amount of oxidizer available, and the remaining fuel can be burned, ramjet-style, in a combustor.

The second clue to the Aurora engine is that witnesses have reported unusual noises in the vicinity of bases where Aurora operates. These include very-low-frequency pulsing sounds, as slow as one pulse per second, and an extremely loud noise on takeoff.

Remarkably, the surging or pulsing sound is associated with a class of standstill-to-hypersonic "combined-cycle" propulsion systems invented in the late 1950s for the Aerospace Plane, which was strikingly similar to the X-30, according to those who worked on it, and concealed since then by obscurity rather than security. Similar engines have been investigated in Russia and Japan.

These powerplants are called "rocket-based combined-cycle" (RBCC) engines. An RBCC engine uses cryogenic fuel and combines features of a ramjet, a rocket, and a turbine engine in an integrated engine that can provide thrust from standstill to Mach 6. It is lighter than a classic turbo-ramjet and delivers higher ISp across the entire speed range than a rocket-ramjet combination.

The RBCC engine is based on a ramjet duct, which incorporates both a fuel injector and a group of small rocket-type nozzles, and a turbine-driven compressor (which is not a turbojet). The methane fuel drives the turbine as it expands from a liquid to a gas, and both the high-pressure air from the compressor and the methane from the turbine are delivered to the rocket nozzles in the ramjet duct. Liquid oxygen (LOX) can be added to the nozzles.

To start the engine, methane is pumped through the aircraft's skin, where it is heated to ambient tempera-

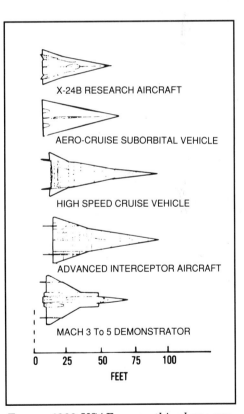

From a 1983 USAF paper, this shows configurations for a variety of hypersonic missions. The high-speed cruise vehicle—a 75-degree delta with an overall length of just under 100 feet—is particularly noteworthy. USAF via David Selegan

ture. The methane expands through the turbine, spinning the compressor and pumping air into the nozzles, where the compressed air-methane mixture is ignited. The high-velocity rocket exhaust draws air through the ramjet duct. As the engine ignites, methane is used to cool the ramjet duct walls. pumping more energy into the turbine.

At idle and low speeds, however, the ramjet duct is too large for the air-flow. The flow becomes discontinuous, with a cyclic build-up and release of pressure in the duct, producing the distinctive noises associated with these unidentified aircraft. The frequency may be as low as one per second and the amplitude is very large, even with a small test engine. "It's the God-awfulest sound you ever heard," says one witness.

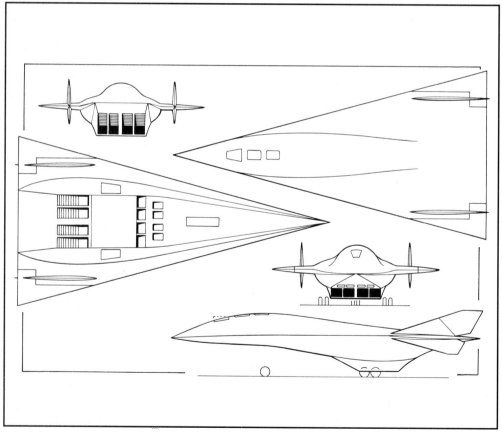

This drawing of Aurora is based on the North Sea eyewitness report and on open-source studies of hypersonic designs. The forebody profile is raised in order to smooth out the increase in cross-sectional area along the vehicle and reduce transonic drag. The bulged underside or "beer belly" results from the use of the entire lower forebody as a compression ramp.

The pulsing is a low-speed phenomenon and has no connection with pulsed detonation wave engine (PDWE) technology, which has been linked to the unusual "doughnut-on-a-rope" contrails that have been seen over the United States. The explanation for these contrails is still not clear.

The RBCC engine needs more thrust for takeoff, climb, and transonic acceleration, so LOX is added to the rocket nozzles. This increases their exhaust velocity and draws more air through the ramjet—in effect, the ramjet thinks it is going faster than the airplane —and thereby increases the pressure ratio to the point where more methane can be added (through the fuel injector) and burned in the duct. The RBCC engine is now running as an air-augmented rocket.

The engine needs less oxygen as the vehicle accelerates, for two main reasons. First, more air is flowing into the ramjet duct; second, increased skin friction and higher duct temperatures mean that the methane driving the turbine has more energy, so the compressor is delivering more air pressure to the rocket nozzles. The LOX flow is gradually reduced and reaches zero at about Mach 2.5.

At higher speeds, the methane supply to the rocket nozzles may be shut down and all the fuel is delivered through the fuel injector. Up to almost Mach 6, the compressor exhaust can continue to supercharge the ramjet—increasing its thrust and ISp. At cruising speed, the compressor inlet closes (the turbine continues to operate, to provide auxiliary power) and the strut with the rocket nozzles retracts to reduce drag in the duct. The engine can then run as a pure ramjet.

Physically, the engines would be installed in multiple modules. Several small ramjets are shorter and lighter than one large duct with the same airflow and thrust potential. The use of the wide underbody as an inlet ramp makes it desirable for the inlet area to be relatively wide and shallow, which is easier to achieve with multiple ducts. One eyewitness to Aurora described it as having "an evil smiley face" underneath.

Professor Paul Czysz, who studied RBCC engines for hypersonic aircraft at McDonnell Douglas, says that their performance is remarkable. A hypersonic aircraft, with combined-cycle engines sized for cruising flight, will have thrust equal to its fully loaded weight on takeoff and in the climb, when the engines are in their rocket mode. With high thrust and low drag, "they go like scalded rabbits," he says. A Marquardt paper, published in 1976, describes a similar engine as a "supercharged ejector ramjet" and credits it with a thrust-to-weight ratio of 25:1—two-and-a-half times that of today's best fighter engines.

Some idea of the potential of these engines can be gained from looking at NASP. Blocky, wide in cross-section, and almost wingless, NASP could not be described as aerodynamically perfect for the Mach 0–2 regime. It weighs at least 350,000 pounds at takeoff, and its body dwarfs the ramjet module inlets. Yet, those engines have enough power to propel NASP to Mach 3.

In its ducted rocket mode, an RBCC engine will be unbelievably noisy. The multiple, small rocket nozzles, with a velocity of many thousands of feet per second, will be mixing in the ducts with slower airflow through the inlets, and the total exhaust will mix with the outside air. The process will generate noise efficiently at many fre-

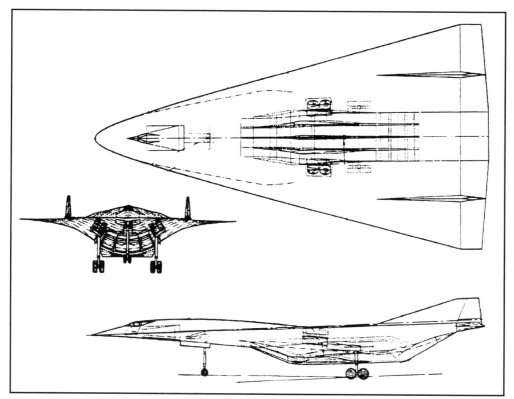

Remarkably, this NASA study was pub-lished one month after the North Sea sighting was first publicized. It is bigger than the Aurora design—it is designed as a strike aircraft with a 10,000–pound weapon load—and uses over-and-under turboramjets rather than lighter com-bined-cycle engines. However, the similari-ties are striking. NASA

quencies, which will interact with one another. Add the fact that the engines could be pushing out almost as much thrust as a 747's engines, and it is easy to see why Aurora "sounds like the sky being ripped open."

Unlike many ramjet-based propulsion schemes, the combined-cycle engine works reasonably well even in level flight at subsonic speeds—when the aircraft is refueling in flight, for instance. In that mode, it is about as efficient as a 1960s technology military turbofan.

There are a number of good reasons why these engines work so well. According to Dr. Fred Billig at the Applied Physics Laboratory of Johns Hopkins University, which experimented with them in the 1960s, one of the attractive features of the combined-cycle engine is that it delivers high thrust per unit of frontal area , which, in the transonic realm, "is more important than many people think." This is because it does not run as a pure ramjet until it is almost at its cruising speed; at takeoff, it is a ducted

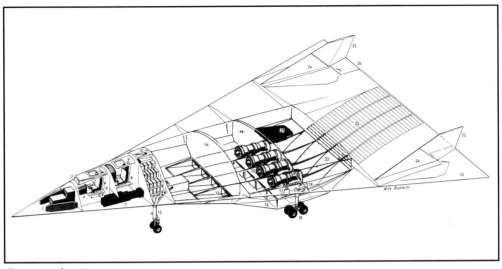

Cutaway drawing

rocket, and it then transitions seamlessly—without any mode or shape changes—into a supercharged ramjet.

The turbo-compressor section of the RBCC is fundamentally different from a turbojet because the compressor and turbine are in separate gas streams. In a turbojet, the air that has been compressed in the inlet and the compressor is extremely hot at high speeds, so that the engine has to be throttled back to keep turbine temperatures within limits. This does not happen in the combined-cycle engine, so the turbo-compressor can run to its maximum capacity throughout the speed range. Also, the capacity of the compressor can be increased by using liquid methane to cool and densify the air that enters the inlet.

Above all, however, the combined-cycle engine is recovering energy that most systems throw away. By using methane to cool the structure, the engines, and the systems, the combined-cycle engine converts the heat gener-

KEY TO CUTAWAY DRAWING	
1	Synthetic-aperture radar antennas
2	Retractable windshield
3	Pilot's ejection seat
4	Instrument console
5	Entry/escape hatch
6	Elevating seat mounting
7	Electro-optical/infra-red cameras, left and right
8	RSO's ejection seat
9	Entry/escape hatch
10	Inflight refueling slipway
11	Main avionics bay
12	Aft-retracting nose landing gear
13	Turbo-compressor inlets (closed at high speeds)
14	Integral tanks for methane and LOX
15	Turbo-compressors
16	Main engine inlets
17	Methane injector strut
18	Main landing gear
19	Methane/air/LOX nozzles
20	Methane turbines
21	Satellite communications antenna
22	Exhaust nozzles
23	Afterbody heat shield
24	Vertical fins
25	Rudders
26	Rotating wing-tip elevons

ated by air friction into mechanical energy (through the methane turbine) and then uses it to supercharge the ramjet, generating additional thrust.

In 1985, McDonnell Douglas proposed a 305-passenger Mach 5 airliner. Designed primarily for the fast-growing air routes between the US and Asia, it became known as the Orient Express—a name later misapplied to NASP by an over-enthusiastic Presidential speechwriter. McDonnell Douglas

The effect is a substantial boost in ISp across the entire speed range.

In this respect, Aurora works exactly like World War II fighters such as the P-51, in which the engine radiator was placed in an aerodynamic duct that functioned as a ramjet and, at high speeds, allegedly produced enough thrust to offset most of the drag of the cooling system.

The RBCC is far from the only engine concept to have been studied for the zero-to-hypersonic mission. The air-turbo-ramjet (ATR) or turbo-rocket dates back to 1949 patents and a version of the concept, the Pratt & Whitney PW304, was designed and built for the Lockheed CL-400 spyplane. The ATR resembles an afterburning turbofan, except that the turbine that drives the fan runs on hot, unburnt hydrogen or methane rather than air. (Japan's IHI Heavy Industries is testing an ATR.) In all these engines, the fan is allowed to windmill at high speeds, so the faster the aircraft goes, the more it behaves like a ramjet.

More recently, Pratt & Whitney has designed a refined version of the ATR, the twin-spool hydrogen expander (TSHE) engine, which dispenses with the complex heat exchanger. Another intriguing engine devised by them is the rocket fan, which is based on the oldest known design for a heat engine: the steam turbine devised by Hero of Alexandria in AD 75. It is similar to the ATR except that there is no turbine, and the fan is driven by tiny rocket nozzles in the blade tips.

There is a chance that some other variation on the many zero-to-hypersonic cycles has been developed and selected for Aurora. A Pratt & Whitney engineer who presented a paper on the TSHE and the rocket fan at a 1985 conference added a gnomic and perhaps

significant comment: "In the course of this work, another interesting cycle came up—but that's another story."

On balance, though, the secrecy that surrounds NASP's engine, the fact that it is partly a ducted rocket, and the Aurora noise reports, all point toward an RBCC solution for both NASP and Aurora, with Rocketdyne, Marquardt, and Pratt & Whitney as the leading candidate contractors.

Propulsion and thermal management are probably the toughest challenges in producing a hypersonic aircraft. Aurora's structure may not be as hard to design and build as the A-12 was in its day. Modern titanium alloys would be adequate for most of the surface and for the substructure.

Throughout its early definition stage, NASP was expected to use new high-temperature titanium-based materials called "intermetallics" for most of its structure. In early 1992, however, the NASP office said that a conventional titanium alloy—Beta-21S— would be adequate, and was already available in production quantities. No known aircraft uses Beta-21S.

Since the SR-71 days, more great strides have been made in the highly heat-resistant materials that are needed for the parts of the vehicle that see stagnation temperatures in the realm of thousands of degrees. Lockheed's experimental hypersonic-glide vehicle used reinforced carbon-carbon (RCC) composites, consisting of carbon fibers in a carbon matrix, formed under heat and pressure, and capable of withstanding temperatures as high as 3,000 degrees Fahrenheit without cooling. These could be used for the leading edges of the wings and inlet, and for the rear underbody.

Aurora's airframe might well incorporate some stealth technology. It

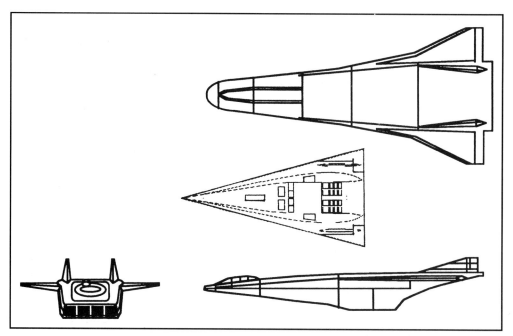

The X-30 NASP differs from Aurora and other hypersonics in having a broader for- *ward fuselage, increasing drag but providing more thrust for acceleration.* USAF

does not need it to survive, but reduced frontal radar cross-section (RCS) might help it to achieve surprise. Clearly, Aurora is going to have an infrared (IR) signature like the rising sun. But most defensive systems do not make use of long-range IR detectors because unless they are airborne, they are useless in cloudy weather. If designers did decide to reduce RCS, they could use the radar-absorbent material (RAM) developed by Lockheed for the F-22's exhaust system, which is based on a ceramic-matrix composite material.

Like the SR-71, Aurora probably has a crew of two: pilot and reconnaissance systems operator (RSO). Flying Aurora will be quite unlike flying a conventional aircraft. There will be little, if any, outside view because a nor-

mal windshield causes too much drag and gets too hot.

There are a number of solutions to the vision problem. Fully synthetic vision, relying on sensors to provide a TV-type picture to the pilot, is distrusted by pilots but is being considered for the next-generation civil supersonic transport. Unlike the Concorde, that aircraft would not have an articulated droop-snoot nose, so it would rely completely on synthetic vision or automatic landing. A more conservative but heavier solution would be a retractable windshield and elevating pilot's seat and controls.

In the cruise, at more than a mile per second, vision is irrelevant. By the time the human eye can see something, it is too late to do anything about it. Instead, the pilot will be a

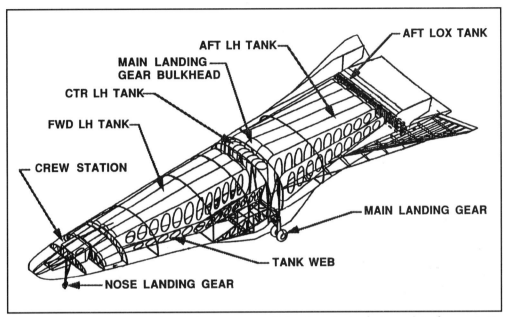

AFT LH TANK

AFT LOX TANK

MAIN LANDING
GEAR BULKHEAD

CTR LH TANK

FWD LH TANK

CREW STATION

MAIN LANDING GEAR

TANK WEB

NOSE LANDING GEAR

Internal view of the X-30 shows that it is put together unlike a conventional airplane, with much of its strength in large, *light, lengthwise webs attached to a single cross-bulkhead level with the landing gear mounts.*

mission manager, monitoring the aircraft and its systems and following the course of the flight on large-format cathode ray tube (CRT) displays. The pilot's most important function will be to cope with the unexpected: differences in upper-air temperature, weather over the target area or the refueling zone, or problems with the systems, for example.

The RSO will supervise a battery of sensors. The most important could be a synthetic-aperture radar (SAR), a side-looking radar that takes a sequence of snapshots of the target as the aircraft moves, and compiles them into a single radar image which is as sharp as it would be if it were acquired using an antenna hundreds of feet wide. The best SAR images are classified, but have been described as "near-photographic," allowing different types of vehicles (tanks or trucks, for instance) to be distinguished easily from more than 100 miles away regardless of clouds or smoke.

In clear weather, Aurora would use daylight and infrared cameras for ultra-detailed work. Thanks to satellite programs, electronic cameras using charge-coupled device (CCD) arrays now achieve equivalent resolution to ultra-fine-grain reconnaissance film; CCDs also have some ability to work in low light levels. A phased-array antenna built into Aurora's upper surface—near the rear end, where heat and ionization would be at a minimum—would allow it to transmit real-time or near-real-time imagery to the Pentagon's satellite network.

NASP is designed to go all the way into orbit, but funding levels are such that it may never fly at all. USAF

This is not a photograph but an image acquired by a synthetic-aperture radar. The radar used here, a Loral UPD-8, is a generation or two older than the high-resolution Hughes and Loral SARs used in the SR-71 and U-2, but all imagery from those radars is highly classified. Loral

On the ground, the digitized imagery is fed into a machine that uses a laser to print the imagery on to film, with results that are indistinguishable, even by experts, from original film loaded directly into the camera. Film is used for the final output because these cameras gather data at such a rapid rate that they will quickly swamp even the vast electronic "juke-box" memories used by the intelligence community. In fact, Aurora could offer an operational advantage over satellites in that it can use film as an alternative to CCDs.

One thing is certain: very little in Aurora's development will have been easy. Former Lockheed chief engineer Clarence "Kelly" Johnson once recalled: "I offered a $50 reward to anyone who could find anything that was easy. Someone came up with a marker that could mark part numbers on titanium. It worked well—but then the part number fell right out of the part." The marker contained a small quantity of chlorine, which is death to titanium. Later, it cost the Air Force $1 million to develop a paint for the USAF stars-and-bars insignia which did not turn brown after the first Mach 3 flight.

Like the A-12 and other high-speed aircraft, Aurora will have presented challenges in thermal management, high-speed propulsion efficiency, and the design of unique subsystems and components to operate at high temperatures. If it does use weapons, or if it is designed so that it can be adapted to launch weapons, new weapon release concepts will be necessary. Some kind of rigidly encapsulated ejection seat will be necessary if safe ejection is required through most of the flight envelope.

Some discussion of Aurora's relationship to NASP, particularly outside the program, has assumed that NASP is a cover for Aurora or a conduit for white-world materials work into the program. In some ways, however, NASP can be seen as an extrapolation of Aurora, which got under way as the results of early Aurora work began to emerge.

Many of NASP's key features represent one significant step beyond Aurora. NASP uses a more exotic, higher-energy fuel: slush hydrogen rather than methane. Aurora, with its tapered, pointed nose, is a cruiser—the shape is a compromise between drag and inlet efficiency. NASP's spatula nose creates more drag and weighs more, but it looks more like what it is, an inlet ramp, because NASP does not cruise in the atmosphere but constantly accelerates. NASP uses a similar engine to Aurora, but adds a supersonic combustion ramjet (scramjet) mode for speeds above Mach 8, and a rocket for the final kick into orbit.

NASP is designed to re-enter the atmosphere with most of its fuel gone, so it makes little use of active cooling and requires a better thermal protection system (TPS) which adds weight. To keep the rest of the structure as light as possible, it uses titanium-matrix composites rather than monolithic titanium.

The USAF's NASP program director, Dr. Robert R. Barthelemy, does not confirm these links, but does not exactly deny them either. As he said in a late 1992 interview: "It's [NASP] involved a lot of people, and we've been very serious about what we've been doing."

"But," he continued, "we've certainly developed certain capabilities that might, right now for all I know, be being used by all kinds of communities. And there may also be some spin-off from some earlier work that's found its way into our activity."

Aurora is not just a spyplane. It is a very important stepping-stone toward real access to space, the kind of access that NASA's civil-service lifers promised from the shuttle but failed to deliver. Unfortunately, one factor above all prevents Aurora's potential from being exploited and prevents its true importance from being recognized.

The US government says that it doesn't exist.

The Price of Denial

When you have eliminated the impossible, whatever remains, however improbable, must be the truth.

—Conan Doyle, *A Study in Scarlet.*

Faced with clear evidence that Aurora exists, in the form of a sighting by a highly qualified witness plus a stream of other reports, the US Air Force has continued to deny that Aurora is real.

"The Air Force has no such program . . . and if such a program existed elsewhere, I'd know about it—and I don't," stormed Bush administration USAF Secretary Donald B. Rice in a letter to the *Washington Post* in December 1992. "The Air Force has no aircraft or aircraft program even remotely similar to the capabilities being attributed to 'Aurora,'" he continued, adding that "the Air Force has never created cover stories to protect any program or vehicle like Aurora."

Rice's denial followed a series of documented observations pointing to a secret, high-speed aircraft program. As well as the North Sea sighting, there were the *Aviation Week* reports and the California booms. There was the lack of controversy over the SR-71 retirement and the upward-spiraling size of the black budget.

Not everybody can be right, and there are a number of hypotheses con-

cerning what might actually be happening in the skies over the United States. Rice's comments suggest that there are no classified, highly supersonic aircraft in existence. If that is the case, then all the eyewitness observations are wildly inaccurate. In the case of the North Sea sighting, the only possible explanation is that the story was an intentional fabrication— an explanation that nobody who has talked to the witness can easily credit. This hypothesis does not address the sonic booms. It requires an alternative explanation for the level of activity at Groom Lake, and the noncontroversial retirement of the SR-71.

Alternatively, secret supersonic aircraft may exist but be very different from the type of system described in this book, with different missions and characteristics; or they may not be operational. This hypothesis covers the California booms and the activity at Groom Lake. But it has a fatal flaw: Rice's denial quite clearly covers all such programs.

Elected officials who would know about Aurora have deftly avoided talk-

Early in 1993, Aerospace Daily *described a secret reconnaissance aircraft project that had allegedly been canceled in 1986. Its description of a B-1-sized, Mach 5 air-craft was oddly reminiscent of this Lockheed artist's impression, released in 1981.* Lockheed

ing about it. I asked Sen. Sam Nunn, chairman of the Senate Armed Services Committee (SASC), about the California booms at a press conference in Dayton, Ohio, in the summer of 1992. Also present was Sen. John Glenn from Ohio, who is a senior member of the Senate Intelligence Committee.

Senator Nunn is briefed on classified military collection programs, including unacknowledged SAPs (Special Access Programs). Normally, the full SASC and intelligence committees—including Senator Glenn—are given the same briefing.

But Steven Aftergood, who edits the *Secrecy and Government Bulletin* for the Federation of American Scientists has reported the existence of a subset of SAPs called "waived programs," in which the secretary of defense waives the requirement to notify

the full committees, and briefs only the chairperson and senior minority member of each committee. If the hypersonic aircraft is a waived program, Nunn would be briefed on it and Glenn would not.

Nunn's response to the question was to refer it immediately to Glenn, without expressly declining to comment. Glenn declined to comment.

Meanwhile, the USAF, through its public affairs offices, has attempted to—as they put it—"debunk" reports of high-speed aircraft. Gen. Walter Hogle, chief of USAF public affairs, even suggested that the unidentified aircraft might have been a Royal Air Force Vulcan bomber, which is not only incapable of refueling from a KC-135 but is almost as big as the tanker, with a three-times-greater wingspan than the unidentified aircraft. Chris Gibson, an expert in aircraft recognition, responds scornfully: "A Vulcan? I think I learned that one when I was three years old."

The service's official response to the North Sea sighting is that the report "will probably remain unchallenged, simply because there is not enough information available to even hazard a guess."

But the report—as published in the British magazine *Jane's Defence Weekly*—includes the precise location of the August 1989 sighting. Gibson does not recall the precise date, but says that it was close to midday, and that the cloud cover was thin and high, a factor which would narrow down the choice of dates.

The magazine also said that the aircraft was refueling from a KC-135 tanker and was accompanied by two F-111 bombers. The USAF has only two F-111 units in Europe, and a single wing of tankers.

Aviation and the military are both notorious for their obsessional record-keeping, but General Hogle said in January 1993 that he did not know if the USAF has attempted to determine which KC-135s and F-111s used AARA (Air-to-Air Refueling Area) 6A during August 1989. Certainly, no Air Force investigator has contacted Chris Gibson, or anyone else involved with the story, in an effort to narrow down the dates of the event.

The question of tanker support brings up another of the many anomalies in USAF statements relating to reconnaissance aircraft. In 1992, Strategic Air Command and Tactical Air Command were merged into Air

Japan's Advanced Space Plane (ASP) project is one of a number of reusable launch- *ers under study worldwide. So far, only rig tests have been undertaken.* Bill Sweetman

Germany's Sanger proposal is a very large two-stage system with a rocket-powered orbiter mounted on a million-pound, Mach 6, *ramjet-powered launcher.* Deutsche Aerospace

Combat Command (ACC); and, at the same time, most of their tankers were transferred to Air Mobility Command. Almost the only exceptions were a few tanker units co-located with bomber wings or the newly formed composite wings.

One tanker unit does not fit the pattern. The 9th Wing at Beale AFB in California still operates the KC-135Q tankers that were specially modified to support the A-12 and the SR-71.

At a conference in early 1993, Gen. Ronald Fogelman, commander of AMC, remarked that the KC-135Qs "belong to Mike Loh [ACC commander Gen. John M. Loh] right now, because they're tied up in support of the U-2 program."

This statement is inaccurate, because the U-2R cannot be refuelled in flight. If the KC-135Qs do not support U-2Rs, what do they support? And why does the commander of AMC, who has overall responsibility for tanker training and support, not know the right answer to that question?

The Air Force has also cast doubt on the seismographic evidence collected since June 1991 by the US Geological Survey (USGS). Under contract to the USAF, Massachusetts Institute of Technology's Lincoln Laboratory analyzed one of these readings and concluded that it was caused by a Navy fighter on an air defense flight-test mission.

This does not explain repeated readings from sensors more than eighty miles inland, unless pilots have been routinely violating the ban on supersonic flight over metropolitan areas. The USAF Flight Test Center states that the boom carpet of an aircraft at 50,000 feet extends only twenty-five miles on either side of the flight path. Booms have been known to propagate over greater distances—but only under unusual conditions, when produced by large aircraft at high altitudes.

Also, witnesses describe the booms as a "rumbling" sound rather than the pop-thud of a fighter boom. "There are a lot of little inconsistencies," says Dr. Jim Mori of the USGS. "If it was just fighters, why didn't they come out and say that the first time it happened?"

Another strange inconsistency is that the Air Force's first statement on the mysterious sonic booms in California referred to an analysis of just one of the boom events, which allegedly matched the boom with the track of "a Navy fighter participating in an air defense flight-test mission." In its later statements, the Air Force claims to have linked all the California boom events to Navy sorties.

Air Force denials cut no ice with researchers in the Netherlands, who have investigated a sonic boom heard over Holland on August 19, 1992. The boom caused property damage and prompted questions from the Dutch parliament to the Ministry of Defence, which found no record of supersonic movements in Dutch airspace.

According to Hein W. Haak of the Royal Netherlands Meteorological Institute, the signal "differs in many aspects" from earthquakes, and resembles a simple chemical explosion in the atmosphere. However, there is no record of any incident that would cause such an explosion.

Records of the booms caused by smaller aircraft such as MiG-29 and MiG-31 fighters have also been studied, but these are too small to cause a substantial boom while remaining outside Dutch airspace, according to one of the researchers.

The Dutch team also investigated the possibility that the boom could have been caused by re-entering space debris or a meteorite, but concluded that the former would not have produced so intense a shock, while a meteorite large enough to cause such a boom would have produced a fireball as bright as the new moon. Their conclusion: the boom was produced by an unidentified supersonic aircraft over the North Sea.

It is not surprising that boom reports are confined to the vicinity of the North Sea and California. Studies suggest that a hypersonic aircraft, cruising above 100,000 feet, would not cause a perceptive sea-level boom. On takeoff, a hypersonic aircraft will climb steeply to its cruising altitude, keeping the boom confined to a relatively small area.

On descent, a long, gradual deceleration within a narrow speed-and-height corridor is critical to maximize range and payload and keep the aircraft within its thermal and structural limits. Therefore, the boom is most likely to be heard during descent to landing—over California or Nevada—or to a refueling rendezvous, as over the North Sea.

The difficulty of pinning down a specific track for the boomer could be attributable to a phenomenon called a "secondary boom." When the Concorde supersonic transport entered service, it was found that the sonic boom from a large aircraft above 60,000 feet could be refracted in the upper atmosphere and cause a disturbance many tens of miles from its source. (Secondary booms, however, have not been associated with small aircraft at fighter-like altitudes.)

The US Air Force's credibility is further undermined by the fact that the Department of Defense explicitly authorizes the dissemination of misleading information in order to protect classified programs. In a supplement to the National Industrial Security Program manual, released in draft form in March 1992, the DoD told contractors how to draft cover stories that "must be believable and cannot reveal any information regarding the true nature of the contract."

Steven Aftergood, of the Federation of American Scientists, comments: "Once we know that the DoD practices this kind of deception, it becomes harder to discern what's for real and what is not."

What could well be such a cover story emerged in early 1993, when unidentified Pentagon and industry sources told trade newsletter *Aerospace Daily* that a top-secret Aurora-type project did exist, but was canceled about 1986 after only drawings and "small models" had been made.

The canceled plane was to have a speed of Mach 4–5, but, a source told the newsletter, "we couldn't make it work." Trying to make the plane's ramjet engines operate at high speed was like "lighting a match in a wind tunnel," another source said. "It's not an easy thing to do, and it hasn't been done yet."

Hypersonic expert Paul Czysz calls such statements nonsense, recalling that McDonnell Aircraft and Johns Hopkins were flying Typhon test vehicles at Mach 5 in 1960. The match-in-a-wind-tunnel analogy "was used in the 1950s, and it wasn't valid then," says Czysz. He recalls that, when he first heard that comparison used, "I was burning hydrogen at 7,000 feet per second" in laboratory tests.

If the *Aerospace Daily* story is correct, moreover, the US government first canceled one aircraft because its best engineers could not make ramjets work properly at Mach 5—and, at the same time, launched a full-scale project to build a plane that would fly four times as fast on ramjet power. The National Aerospace Plane (NASP) was given President Reagan's blessing in February 1986, with the aim of flying a prototype all the way into orbit in the early 1990s.

The idea that the US government may be engaged in such "disinformation" efforts may be unpalatable, but there are all too many reasons why it is far from incredible. The use of cover stories to conceal the A-12, described in the introduction, is one example. Outside the defense world, the number of government officials who have been caught in attempts to deceive their superiors or Congress is staggering—and they are only the ones who got caught.

"The State Department only lied to me a couple of hundred times," recalls a former member of the Senate.

Often, he says, they did so when they felt trapped: if they were faced with a direct question, a "no comment" was tantamount to a confirmation. "At that point, they might as well announce it to the press," he adds.

The cost of such secrecy is measured in dollars as well as in official credibility. Lockheed's Ben Rich estimates that 10–15 percent of the cost of a Special Access Program is spent on security. It goes for special secure facilities, special procedures, the time that new hires spend cooling their heels on full pay while their clearances are reviewed, and the extra cost of working at Groom Lake rather than Palmdale or Edwards.

Add missed opportunities to the price. There is a worldwide need for a space launch system to do what the shuttle was supposed to do: provide regular access to space at an affordable cost. A number of countries are working on the problem in different ways.

Germany's Deutsche Aerospace is investigating the Sanger vehicle, named after the visionary designer of the skip-bomber. Sanger is a two-stage winged vehicle: a giant, million-pound, Mach 6 carrier aircraft powered by turbo-ramjet engines, carrying a smaller rocket-powered top stage. Sanger would probably work, and would be quite flexible, but the massive first stage will be expensive.

British Aerospace (BAe) made a splash in the early 1980s with its Horizontal Take-Off and Landing (HOTOL) vehicle. BAe based its original plans on the Rolls-Royce RB.545 engine, which was designed to use liquid hydrogen to cool and densify atmospheric air in a heat exchanger. The high-pressure hydrogen from the heat exchanger drove a compressor that fed the air to a rocket chamber.

Another Japanese spaceplane project is HOPE (H2 Orbiting Plane), a 33,000-pound, unpiloted, reusable space transporter capable of delivering or retrieving orbital payloads. Kawasaki

BAe expected the 440,000 pound HOTOL to orbit a 15,000 pound payload after taking off from a trolley. Further studies showed that BAe had been optimistic about the weight and efficiency of the engine, and that the payload was in fact marginal.

More recently, BAe has worked with the Ukraine's Antonov design bureau to develop a pure-rocket, air-launched vehicle weighing some 500,000 pounds. It would be carried to altitude by Antonov's monster An-225—the world's largest aircraft. The An-225 is a stretched, six-engine version of the An-124 heavy cargo transport and was designed to carry the Soviet Buran space shuttle. The air-launched HOTOL is a relatively low-risk approach, but its sheer size—the complete vehicle weighs close to a million and a half pounds—is daunting.

Japan's National Aerospace Laboratory (NAL) is studying a single-stage Advanced Spaceplane which would use a liquid-air-cycle engine (LACE), not unlike the HOTOL engine, for takeoff and acceleration to hypersonic speeds, and scramjets from Mach 6 to near-orbital speeds. It would be fueled by slush hydrogen. The problem here is that LACE has always been considered a high risk, and the efficiency of the entire densification and liquefaction process is critical. The NAL has some LACE demonstration work under way.

The US National Aerospace Plane still looks like a strong contender. It has the most advanced technology and lowest projected weight of any concept—the NASP program office still believes that it can build an operational NASP, with a useful payload, that weighs only 600,000 pounds. But its performance is dependent on scramjet efficiency, which is impossible to determine without flight-tests.

The problem facing all these spaceplane projects is money. NASP, which was the best funded of all of them, has already been cut back and may face cancellation because of a lack of support from NASA.

On December 2, 1992, midway through the Fourth Annual Aerospace Planes conference in Orlando, Florida, the shuttle *Discovery* lifted off with a classified payload. But not everyone was cheering. The cost of the launch was equivalent to one year's funding for all the spaceplane projects discussed in Orlando, most of which are expected to run out of money by 1995.

"The launch we saw this morning, although most people are afraid to recognize it, cost $500 million," says John Swihart, veteran Boeing engineer and president of the National Center for Advanced Technologies (NCAT). "That's ludicrous. That's something we can't continue to do. We've got to think of a better way."

The answer, given the budgets that all the nations involved are likely to see in the 1990s, is international collaboration. But Aurora casts a permanent shadow over any negotiations. Europeans are convinced that NASP is a cover for Aurora, and that the United States is not serious about the spaceplane business. The US government has an unfortunate history of initiating collaborative programs, and then pulling out because a parallel black program shows more promise.

The Europeans are also convinced that NASP will not work, on the basis of their own studies of NASP-type vehicles. But their designs are based on turbo-ramjet engines rather than combined-cycle powerplants, which are lighter and provide higher average ISp.

It is entirely possible that not all the news about Aurora is good. Secrecy has often been a cover for technical and financial problems, or for activities that have outlived their usefulness. It is conceivable that Aurora has missed performance targets—the Blackbird, brilliant as it was, never made its design range. Aurora may have overrun its projected costs or it may be designed and equipped in such a way that it is dedicated to an obsolete nuclear warfighting mission. Sooner or later, that story will come out.

Opening up Aurora would accomplish several things. It would clear the air for spaceplane collaboration. It might convince NASA and the Europeans that there is a case for pursuing a single-stage-to-orbit system based on RBCC engines and scramjets. And it would give the NASP community access to an excellent high-speed test vehicle.

Nothing thrives in the dark, except ghosts, mushrooms, and bad decisions.

Dyna-Soar II—a Lockheed study for a lift-ing-body-type mini-shuttle, primarily de- *signed to return crews from the Space Sta-tion in an emergency.* Lockheed

Index

A-12 Oxcart, 6, 8, 9, 10, 15, 17, 25, 27-28, 39, 44-46
Aftergood, Steven, 88, 92
Air Launched Sortie Vehicle, 55-56, 58
Air-to-Air Refueling Area 6A, 15, 89
Anti-Satellite System, 22-23
ASM-135 system, 20
Air-turbo-ramjet, 79, 81

B-1B, 25, 48
B-2, 22, 23, 26, 28
B-52, 66
B-58, 10, 48
Barthelemy, Robert R., 86
Beale AFB, 47, 90
Billig, Dr. Fred, 78
Boost Glide Research Vehicle, 53
Brass Bell, 36
Bredt, Irene, 33

Carter, President Jimmy, 29
Challenger, 21
CIA, 6, 8, 9, 10, 15, 24-25, 27, 28, 29, 45
CL-400, 8, 37, 48, 70, 79
Concorde, 64, 68
Crossfield, Scott, 34
Curtiss-Wright, 40, 42
Czysz, Paul, 24, 77, 92

D-21 drone, 9, 39-40, 44, 46, 65-66, 72
Deutsche Aerospace, 93
Dornberger, Dr. Walter, 33
Douglas D-558, 34
Douglas X-3, 32
Dugan, Gen. Michael, 19
Dyna-Soar, 36, 38-40, 46, 56, 95
Edwards AFB, 7, 13
Eisenhower, President Dwight D., 15, 44

F-111, 15, 89
F-117 stealth fighter, 13, 28
Feltz, Charles, 34
Flight Dynamics Laboratory, 50, 52-54, 60
Francillon, Rene, 56

Galveston Key, 12, 14
Gibson, Chris, 12, 13, 14, 15, 63, 88, 89
Glenn, Sen. John, 88
Goldwater, Barry, 31
Groom Lake, 6, 7, 8, 12-13, 87, 93
Hard Mobile Launcher, 29
Horizontal Take-Off and Landing Vehicle, 93
Horner, Gen. Charles A, 20, 22
Hughes, 85
Hypersonic glide vehicle, 23

Johnson, Clarence L., 31, 86
Johnson, President Lyndon, 8

Kardong, Abe, 31
KC-135, 71, 89
Kennedy, President John F., 49
KH-11 optical satellite, 17-19
KH-12, 21, 23

Lacrosse radar satellite, 17
Lockheed Advanced Development Company, 27, 74
Lockheed Missiles and Space Company, 21, 23
Lockheed Skunk Works, 15, 25, 27, 47, 70
Loh, Gen. John M., 90
Loral, 85
LTV, 20, 38
M2-F1 lifting body, 51
M2-F2 lifting body, 51, 52

Machrihanish, Scotland, 13
Maneuvering Re-entry Research Vehicle, 54, 60, 63
Marquardt RJ43, 41, 45
Marquardt, Roy, 40
Martin-Marietta, 17, 21
McDonnell Douglas, 24, 67, 71, 77, 80
McNamara, Robert, 49
Midgetman missile, 28
MiG-25, 6, 10, 48
MiG-29, 91
MiG-31, 91
Milstar system, 22-23, 26
Mori, Dr. Jim, 91

NACA, 7, 33
NASA, 21, 51, 52
National Aerospace Plane, 66, 67, 74-75, 77, 80, 81, 84, 86, 92, 94
National Hypersonic Flight Research Facility, 54
National Reconnaissance Office, 17, 21, 24, 28, 29
National Security Agency, 17, 24, 28
North Sea sighting, 87, 89
Northrop Corporation, 51
Nunn, Sen. Sam, 88

Perry, Dr. William, J., 29
Pike, John, 28
Pratt & Whitney, 8, 37, 58, 81

RAF Lankenheath, 7
Randolph, Bernard, 19
Reagan, President Ronald, 22, 92
Republic XF-103, 35
Rice, Donald B., 87
Rich, Ben, 15, 47, 93
Royal Observer Corps, 13, 15
Rocket-Based Combined-Cycle engines, 75, 77, 79, 81
Rocketdyne LR-105, 53
Rockwell, 57, 59

SAMOS, 40
Sanger, Eugene, 33, 90, 93
Sputnik 1, 36
SR-71 Blackbird, 4, 5, 6, 9, 11, 13-19, 23-25, 27, 28, 31, 64-65, 68, 69, 71, 73, 85, 87
Storms, Harrison, 34
Synthetic-Aperture Radar, 82-83, 85

Thiokol XLR-99, 53
Titan IV rocket, 17, 21
Transatmospheric Vehicle, 60-63
Trident D-5 missile, 22, 23
TRW, 17
Twin-Spool Hydrogen Expander Engine, 81
Typhon missile, 43

U-2, 7, 44-45, 85
US Geological Service, 11, 91
USAF 5, 19, 33, 49, 91

Weiner, Tim, 28

X-15, 34-36, 39-40, 41, 43, 46, 53
X-20, 46
X-24A, 51
X-24C, 52, 53-54
XB-70, 10, 38, 44
XF-99 Bomarc, 41
XF-103, 36, 41-42
XSM-64, 34

YF-12, 8-9, 49